English Grammar: Step by Step

Written by Elizabeth Weal
Illustrated by Amy Zhang

Tenaya Press
Palo Alto, CA

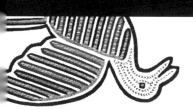

For my students

All inquiries should be addressed to
Elizabeth Weal
Tenaya Press
3481 Janice Way
Palo Alto, CA 94303

650-494-3941
ElizabethWeal@tenaya.com
http://TenayaPress.Tenaya.com

Book design: Stuart Silberman
Cover: Beth Zonderman
Layout: Renée Cook

About the cover

The cover is a photograph of a portion of a mola. Molas are part of the traditional dress of the Central American Cuna (or Kuna) tribe of the San Blas Islands, a chain of tropical islands along the Atlantic coast of Panama. Molas, which also can be found in Colombia, are hand made using a "reverse appliqué" technique. Several layers of different-colored cloth are sewn together; the design is then formed by cutting parts of each layer away.

ISBN 978-0-9796128-7-9

Contents

Welcome

A note to students

Welcome to *English Grammar: Step by Step 1*, a book that will teach you everything you need to understand the basics of English grammar.

The assumption behind this book is that anyone can learn English grammar, regardless of their level of education. To ensure that this occurs, grammar concepts are presented in a step-by-step fashion, starting at the most basic level. Each new concept is followed by exercises that give you the opportunity to practice what you've learned and additional exercises at the end of each chapter provide even more practice. All of the answers to the exercises are in an appendix, so you can check your work as you go. A dictionary of all the words used in this book is included in the back of the book, making it easy to look up words you don't know how to spell. The dictionary also includes pronunciation.

This book also is intended for people who can speak English, but have no formal training writing it. Toward that end, it covers basic concepts like English capitalization and punctuation, topics that often are a mystery to people who never studied English in school. When you finish this book, you can move on to *English Grammar: Step by Step 2* where you'll learn about present tense verbs and prepositions.

Keep in mind that the focus of this book is exclusively on grammar. Learning English requires many other skills in addition to grammar, such as pronunciation, listening comprehension, vocabulary development, and so on. At the same time, if you who want to advance in English you'll need a solid foundation in basic grammar, which is precisely what this book provides.

A note to teachers

English Grammar: Step by Step 1 was written to help Spanish-speaking students learn grammar in a simple, straightforward manner. It assumes no prior knowledge of either English or Spanish grammar and is appropriate for students with only minimal formal education. It also is intended for students who have some knowledge of spoken English, but have minimal experience with the written word. Teachers can use this book as a classroom text in classes with only Spanish-speakers or as a supplement for Spanish-speaking students in mixed-language classes. It also can be made available to students in distance learning programs and in school bookstores that stock ESL materials.

When your students finish this book, they can move on to *English Grammar: Step by Step 2*, a book that uses precisely the same format as this book to teach students about present tense verbs and prepositions.

Because the book is available in English and Spanish, teachers who don't speak Spanish can read the English version to learn some basic differences between English and Spanish grammar, then make the Spanish version of the book available to their students. The English version of this book can also be used by intermediate-level ESL students who want to review fundamental English grammar.

Acknowledgements

Many people gave me the support and encouragement I needed to write this book. My friend and colleague Maria Kleczewska read early drafts and offered invaluable comments based on her teaching experience. This book is much improved from its initial incarnation thanks to her input. My friend Lisa Swagerty took the time to listen to my concerns. Barb Hooper gave me much-needed marketing advice. Gabriela Urricariet was a skilled and thorough editor and translator. Julie Reis helped me find errors others had missed. Amy Zhang created the fanciful illustrations. Book designer Stuart Silberman transformed this manuscript from a sea of gray into a document that's both easy to use and inviting to read. Renée Cook deserves credit for transforming Stuart's design into a polished document. Beth Zonderman created a book cover that made a seemingly dull subject come alive. Finally, I want to thank my friend Mary Bender who opened my eyes to the beauty of Latin American textiles in general and to molas in particular. A mola from her collection is pictured on the cover of this book.

I also want to thank the many Sequoia Adult School staff members—including Barbara Hooper, Lionel De Maine, Pat Cocconi, Ana Escobar, Soledad Rios, Maria Ibarra, and Juan Ramirez—who have supported my efforts and helped make my books available to Sequoia Adult School students.

My amazing husband Bruce Hodge helped with countless tasks, from design assistance to 24/7 technical support while my daughters Chelsea and Caroline offered valuable editorial input. Finally, I want to thank the hundreds of students who inspired me with their enthusiasm for learning and heartfelt dedication to mastering the intricacies of English grammar. Without them, this book never would have been written.

Chapter 1

I am from Mexico.

Learning a language is like building a building. You start at the bottom and work your way up. In this chapter you'll be introduced to the basic building blocks of language: nouns, pronouns, and verbs. You'll also learn how to use the verb **to be** (ser and estar), the most common verb in the English language. Finally, you'll use what you have learned to write simple sentences in English.

At the end of this chapter you will be able to

- identify nouns.
- distinguish between singular and plural nouns.
- recite the subject pronouns in English.
- use the verb **to be** (ser and estar).
- write a sentence in English that tells where you are from.

When you were a baby, the first words you said were most likely the names of people and objects around you. These words, such as mamá and pelota, are called ***nouns***. A ***noun*** is a person, place, animal, or thing. For example,

- ▶ maestra is a noun that is a person.

- ▶ parque is a noun that is a place.

- ▶ elefante is a noun that is an animal.

- ▶ mesa is a noun that is a thing.

In Spanish, nouns are distinguished by gender, either masculine or feminine. For example, la casa is a feminine noun; el parque is a masculine noun. In English, the only nouns that are feminine or masculine refer to certain people and animals. For example, **father** (padre) is a masculine noun and **mother** (madre) is a feminine noun. Only a few English nouns are masculine or feminine. This is good news if you are learning English because it means that you rarely need to think about whether a noun is masculine or feminine!

Using the

The most common word in the English language is **the**. In Spanish, there are four words for **the**: el, la, los, and las. In English, it's easy: you always use **the**.

A noun can either be ***singular*** or ***plural***. A *singular noun* refers to one person, place, animal, or thing. A *plural noun* refers to more than one. The following table gives you examples of how to use **the** with singular nouns. Study these words. You will use them in the exercise on the next page.

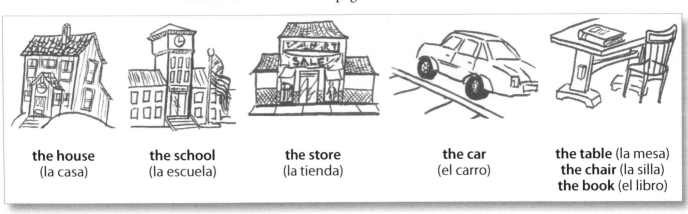

| **the house** (la casa) | **the school** (la escuela) | **the store** (la tienda) | **the car** (el carro) | **the table** (la mesa) **the chair** (la silla) **the book** (el libro) |

Vocabulary: Singular nouns

the student (el estudiante, la estudiante)	**the teacher** (el maestro, la maestra)
the girl (la niña)	**the boy** (el niño)
the sister (la hermana)	**the brother** (el hermano)

1.1.a Directions: Read the sentence in Column 1. In Column 2, write each noun in the sentence. The first question is done for you.

Column 1	Column 2 List each noun in the sentence.
1. Laura tiene un perro y dos gatos.	1a. Laura 1b. perro 1c. gatos
2. Me gusta comer arroz y frijoles.	2a. 2b.
3. Veo una paloma en el jardín.	3a. 3b.
4. Los estudiantes están en el aula.	4a. 4b.
5. La casa es grande.	5a.
6. Miguel y Ernesto son amigos.	6a. 6b. 6c.
7. El lápiz está en la mesa.	7a. 7b.
8. Juan vive en Chicago.	8a. 8b.

1.1.b Directions: Translate these phrases. Use the word list on the previous page. The first two are done for you.

1. la silla	the chair	7. la casa	
2. la tienda	the store	8. la estudiante	
3. el libro		9. la escuela	
4. la niña		10. el carro	
5. la mesa		11. el niño	
6. la maestra		12. el maestro	

1.2   Singular and Plural Nouns

As you learned in the previous section, nouns can be singular or plural. A *singular noun* refers to one person, place, animal, or thing. A *plural noun* refers to more than one person, place, animal, or thing. In both Spanish and English, you usually make a noun plural by adding **s**.

Plant (planta) is a singular noun.

Plant**s** (plantas) is a plural noun.

Book (libro) is a singular noun.

Books (libros) is a plural noun.

Study the singular and plural nouns in the following table. Notice that each plural noun ends with **s**. Notice also that in English you use the same word, **the**, whether the noun that follows is singular or plural.

Singular nouns	Plural nouns
the house (la casa)	**the houses** (las casas)
the school (la escuela)	**the schools** (las escuelas)
the store (la tienda)	**the stores** (las tiendas)
the car (el carro)	**the cars** (los carros)
the table (la mesa)	**the tables** (las mesas)
the chair (la silla)	**the chairs** (las sillas)
the book (el libro)	**the books** (los libros)
the student (el estudiante, la estudiante)	**the students** (los estudiantes, las estudiantes)
the teacher (el maestro, la maestra)	**the teachers** (los maestros, las maestras)

In English you sometimes make nouns plural by adding **es** or **ies**, instead of **s**. You'll learn more about these plural nouns later in this book.

1.2.a Directions: Write S after the noun if it is singular and P after the noun if it is plural. The first two are done for you.

1. the student	S	9. the houses		17. the cat (gato)	
2. the students	P	10. the house		18. the cats	
3. the nurse		11. the book		19. the sister	
4. the nurses		12. the books		20. the sisters	
5. the teachers		13. the chairs		21. the schools	
6. the teacher		14. the chair		22. the school	
7. the dog (perro)		15. the table			
8. the dogs		16. the tables			

1.2.b Directions: Make each noun plural. The first one is done for you.

1. the nurse	the nurses	7. the book	
2. the teacher		8. the house	
3. the student		9. the car	
4. the store		10. the table	
5. the dog		11. the school	
6. the chair		12. the brother	

1.2.c Directions: Translate each phrase into English. The first two are done for you.

1. la mesa	the table	10. las maestras	
2. las mesas	the tables	11. la madre	
3. el perro		12. las casas	
4. los hermanos		13. los carros	
5. los gatos		14. el estudiante	
6. las sillas		15. la estudiante	
7. la maestra		16. las estudiantes	
8. los libros		17. los estudiantes	
9. la silla		18. las hermanas	

To learn a new language, you need to think about how your native language functions; then apply that information to the language you're learning. In this section, you'll learn how to identify verbs and subjects in Spanish sentences. In the next section, you'll learn how to use verbs and subjects in English.

> 👁 **¡Cuidado!** Even though you're eager to learn about English grammar (as opposed to Spanish grammar), don't skip this section. If you do, you'll be confused later on.

A *verb* is a word that shows action. For example, bailar, hablar, and nadar are all verbs. But the most common verbs in Spanish, ser and estar, don't show any action at all. They simply tell the current state of things.

The *subject* of a sentence is usually the first noun in the sentence. The subject tells who or what the sentence is about. The verb usually comes immediately after the subject. Consider this sentence:

▸ Gabriela es maestra.

The verb is es. To identify the subject, look for the first noun in the sentence. As you can see, it's Gabriela. Notice that Gabriela comes immediately before the verb, es.

Now, consider this sentence:

▸ Las casas son grandes.

The verb is son. The first noun in the sentence, casas, is the subject. Here again, the subject comes immediately before the verb.

There are many sentences where the first noun in the sentence is not the subject of the sentence and where the noun does not come immediately before the verb, but you won't be studying those types of sentences until you've mastered more grammar.

Here are more examples of complete sentences. In each example, the subject is <u>underlined</u> and the verb is in **bold**.

▸ <u>Carlos</u> **es** médico.

▸ <u>Los edificios</u> **son** muy grandes.

▸ <u>Mis hermanas</u> **están** en Puebla.

▸ <u>Ángel</u> **está** muy guapo.

1.3.a Directions: The subject of each sentence is underlined. Write **S** if the subject is singular and **P** if the subject is plural. The first two are done for you.

1. <u>El estudiante</u> es de Texas. S

2. <u>Los estudiantes</u> ahora están en Nueva York. P

3. <u>Isabel y yo</u> somos amigas. _____

4. <u>La maestra</u> está en el aula. _____

5. <u>Las sillas</u> son nuevas. _____

6. <u>El vecindario</u> es peligroso. _____

7. <u>El carro</u> siempre está roto. _____

8. <u>Los estudiantes</u> todavía están cansados. _____

9. <u>Yo</u> soy de Los Ángeles. _____

10. <u>Nosotros</u> somos estudiantes nuevos. _____

11. <u>Jennifer López</u> es actriz. _____

12. <u>Las montañas</u> son muy altas. _____

13. <u>Las mujeres</u> están en el teatro. _____

14. <u>Nosotros</u> somos de Brasil. _____

15. <u>La tienda</u> está cerrada. _____

16. <u>Yo</u> estoy enfermo. _____

1.3.b Directions: Put one line under the subject. Put two lines under the verb, ser or estar. The first two are done for you.

1. <u>El estudiante</u> <u>es</u> de Texas.

2. <u>Ellos</u> <u>están</u> en Nueva York.

3. Nosotras somos amigas.

4. La maestra está en el aula.

5. Las sillas son nuevas.

6. El vecindario es peligroso.

7. El carro está roto.

8. Los estudiantes están cansados.

9. Yo soy de Los Ángeles.

10. Alex y yo somos estudiantes nuevos.

11. Jennifer López es actriz.

12. Las montañas son muy altas.

13. Las mujeres están en el teatro.

14. Enrique y yo somos de Brasil.

15. Los perros están en el parque.

16. Los libros están en el suelo.

17. La tienda está cerrada.

18. Lucas está enfermo.

You have learned that the subject of a sentence is the word or words that tell who or what the sentence is about. Read this sentence:

▶ Jorge es de Nicaragua.

The subject of the sentence is Jorge.

A *pronoun* is a word that you can use to replace a noun. A *personal pronoun* is a pronoun that takes the place of a noun that is the subject. For example, instead of saying

▶ Jorge es de Nicaragua.

you can replace Jorge with the pronoun él. The new sentence is

▶ **Él** es de Nicaragua.

Similarly, instead of saying

▶ **Los niños** están en el parque.

you might say

▶ **Ellos** están en el parque.

The following are subject pronouns in English and Spanish.*

| **I** (yo) | **he** (él) | **she** (ella) | **you** (tú, usted, ustedes) | **we** (nosotros, nosotras) | **they** (ellos, ellas) |

*The pronoun **it** cannot be easily translated into Spanish. You'll learn about **it** in the next chapter.

English vs. Spanish: In English, the pronoun **you** is used for tú, usted and ustedes. That means that you'll use the same pronoun whether you're talking to a child or the President of the United States! You'll also use **you** when you are talking to one person and when you are talking to a group of people. Consider these examples:

English	Spanish
You are from Peru.	**Tú** eres de Perú.
You are from Peru.	**Usted** es de Perú.
You are from Peru.	**Ustedes** son de Perú.

English vs. Spanish: In English the pronoun **they** means both ellos and ellas. In other words, **they** is used to refer to a group of males, a group of females, or a group of males and females that you're not part of. Similarly, the pronoun **we** means both nosotros and nosotras, so it can be used to refer to you and one or more males or females.

1.4.a Directions: Translate these subject pronouns from English to Spanish. The first one is done for you.

1. they   ellos   ellas   4. we _____ _____

2. he _____   5. you _____ _____ _____

3. I _____   6. she _____

1.4.b Directions: Use the clue to fill in the correct English pronoun. The first one is done for you.

1. You use this pronoun to talk about a man.   he

2. You use this pronoun to talk about a woman. _____

3. You use this pronoun to talk about yourself. _____

4. You use this pronoun to talk about a group of men, a group of women, or a group of men and women that you are not a part of. _____

5. You use this pronoun to talk about you and one or more other people. _____

6. You use this pronoun to talk about the person you are talking to. _____

1.4.c Directions: Translate these subject pronouns from Spanish to English. The first one is done for you.

1. ella   she   6. usted _____

2. tú _____   7. yo _____

3. él _____   8. ustedes _____

4. ella _____   9. nosotros _____

5. ellas _____   10. ellos _____

1.4.d Directions: Write the subject pronoun—**he**, **she** or **they**—that you can substitute for each noun. The first two are done for you.

Noun	Pronoun	Noun	Pronoun
1. Emma	she	9. the sister	
2. Mario	he	10. the sisters	
3. Nina and Marco		11. the brother	
4. Fred, Tom, and Dan		12. the brothers	
5. the girl		13. the students	
6. the girls		14. Anna	
7. the boys		15. Eduardo	
8. Lucas		16. Sharon and Frank	

1.5   Introducing the Verb *To Be*

The most common verbs in Spanish are ser and estar. In English when you want to use a verb that means either ser or estar you use the verb **to be**. What's confusing is that you <u>never</u> say, **I be, you be**, or **he be**. Instead, you say **I am, you are, he is** and so on. The remainder of this chapter focuses on this important verb. To begin, study this table.

Conjugating the verb to be: Part 1	
I am	yo soy, yo estoy

Notice the following:

▶ The English phrase that means **I am** has two translations: yo soy and yo estoy.

▶ When using the verb **to be,** you always use **am** after the pronoun **I**.

Read this conversation:

*¡De dónde eres?   **Yo soy de México. Soy de México.

Here are some important things to notice about this conversation:

▶ Your response <u>must</u> include the subject pronoun, **I**. This is different from Spanish where the subject pronoun, **yo**, is optional. This sentence is correct:

I am from Peru.

This sentence is not correct:

~~Am from Peru.~~

▶ The English word for de is **from**.

▶ Specific geographic locations are capitalized. Thus **Mexico** always starts with a capital **M**.

▶ All statements in English <u>must</u> begin with a capital letter and end with a period.

Punctuation is very important in English. In fact, if you don't use correct punctuation, people may think you're not very well-educated, even if you are! Thus, when you write sentences in English, make sure that you begin every sentence with a capital letter and end every statement with a period. You'll learn more about English punctuation as you continue in this book.

1.5.a Directions: Rewrite these sentences with correct capitalization and punctuation. Remember that the names of specific locations must begin with a capital letter. The first one is done for you.

1. he is from san luis potosi   He is from San Luis Potosi.

2. linda is from zacatecas

3. anna is from nicaragua

4. peter is from ecuador

5. jesus is from cuba

6. wendy is from chihuahua

7. dulce is from guerrero

8. francisco is from santiago

9. gabriela is from hidalgo

10. edgar is from the usa

1.5.b Directions: One of the sentences in each pair is not a correct sentence. Cross out the **incorrect** sentence. The first one is done for you.

1a. I am from Bolivia.	1b. ~~I from Bolivia.~~
2a. I from New York.	2b. I am from New York.
3a. My from is Puerto Rico.	3b. I am from Puerto Rico.
4a. I from Guatemala.	4b. I am from Guatemala.
5a. I am from Seattle.	5b. Am from Seattle.
6a. I from Ecuador.	6b. I am from Ecuador.
7a. Am de Mexico.	7b. I am from Mexico.

1.5.c Directions: Translate these sentences. Make sure to begin every sentence with a capital letter; capitalize the names of countries, cities, and states; and end every sentence with a period. When you check your work, make sure that each of your sentences is exactly the same as the sentence in Appendix A in the back of this book. The first one is done for you.

1. Yo soy de San Salvador.   I am from San Salvador.

2. Soy de San Salvador.

3. Yo soy de Honduras.

4. Yo soy de Chiapas.

5. Soy de Chiapas.

Using *To Be* with *He* and *She*

You now know how to tell someone where you're from, but suppose you want to talk about the place of origin of your sister or your friend? To do that, you need to use the verb **to be** with **he** or **she** or a noun that you use instead of **he** and **she**. To begin, study this table:

Conjugating the verb to be: Part 2		
he <u>is</u>	él es	él está
Marco <u>is</u>	Marco es	Marco está
the boy <u>is</u>	el niño es	el niño está
she <u>is</u>	ella es	ella está
Maria <u>is</u>	María es	María está
the girl <u>is</u>	la niña es	la niña está

Notice the following:

- ▶ Each English phrase has two translations: one that includes a form of the verb ser and one that includes a form of the verb estar.

- ▶ When using the verb **to be**, you always use **is** after the pronouns **he** and **she** and after nouns that refer to one person.

Study the following sentences:

*Él es de Cuba. **Ella es de Perú.*

It is not correct to say

- ▶ ~~Is from Mexico.~~

1.6.a Directions: Complete each sentence using **am** or **is**. The first two are done for you.

1. I __am__ from Mexico.

2. Lucy __is__ from Peru.

3. Lucinda _____ from New York.

4. Robert _____ from Guatemala.

5. My teacher _____ from Morelia.

6. He _____ from Mexico.

7. She _____ from Puerto Rico.

8. I _____ from Toluca.

9. The boy _____ from Escatepec.

10. I _____ from Havana.

1.6.b Directions: Rewrite the sentence by replacing the underlined words with **he** or **she**. The first one is done for you.

1. <u>The boy</u> is from Los Angeles.   He is from Los Angeles.

2. <u>The girl</u> is from Managua.   _____

3. <u>Ana</u> is from Bogota.   _____

4. <u>My sister</u> is from San Jose.   _____

5. <u>Ramon</u> is from the United States.   _____

1.6.c Directions: One of the sentences in each pair is not a correct sentence. Cross out the **incorrect** sentence. The first one is done for you.

1a. She is from England.   1b. ~~She am from England.~~

2a. I is from New York.   2b. I am from New York.

3a. Is from Miami.   3b. Juan is from Miami.

4a. He is from Chicago.   4b. Is from Chicago.

5a. Am from Santo Domingo.   5b. I am from Santo Domingo.

1.6.d Directions: Translate these sentences. The first one is done for you. Make sure you start each sentence with a capital letter and end each sentence with a period. When you check your work, make sure that each of your sentences is exactly the same as the sentence in the Answers section in the back of this book.

1. Susan es de El Salvador.   Susan is from San Salvador.

2. Juan es de Michoacán.   _____

3. Mi hermano es de Leon.   _____

4. Él es de Guadalajara.   _____

5. Yo soy de Oaxaca.   _____

6. El niño es de San Juan.   _____

1.7   More About the Verb *To Be*

In the last section, you learned how to use the verb **to be** with the pronouns **I, he** and
she. But what form of this verb do you use with all the other pronouns? Study this
table to find out.

Conjugating the verb **to be**: Part 3	
you <u>are</u>	tú eres, tú estás, usted es, usted está, ustedes son, ustedes están
we <u>are</u>	nosotros somos, nosotros estamos
Bob and I <u>are</u>	Bob y yo somos, Bob y yo estamos
they <u>are</u>	ellos son, ellos están, ellas son, ellas están
the boys <u>are</u>	los niños son, los niños están
the girls <u>are</u>	las niñas son, las niñas están

After looking at this table, you can see that, when using the verb **to be,** you use the
verb **are** after the pronouns **you, we** and **they** or after nouns that refer to you and one
other person or to a group of people that doesn't include you.

English vs. Spanish: Remember that the pronoun **you** refers to tú, usted, and
ustedes. That means that you'll say **you are** in each of these situations:
  ▸ **You are** from Sonora. (**Eres** de Sonora o **Tú eres** de Sonora.)
  ▸ **You are** from Sonora. (**Usted es** de Sonora.)
  ▸ **You are** from Sonora. (**Ustedes son** de Sonora.)

English vs. Spanish: In Spanish, you can omit the pronoun that comes before the verb
if the meaning of the sentence is clear without the pronoun. For example, in Spanish
you can say
  ▸ Tú eres de Guatemala. o Eres de Guatemala.
    In English, you <u>must</u> include the pronoun. Thus you must say
  ▸ You are from Guatemala.

Grammar Summary

When to use the verb **to be** (ser o estar):
  ▸ use **am** after the pronoun **I**.
  ▸ use **are** after the pronouns **you, we** and **they**.
  ▸ use **is** after the pronouns **he** and **she**.

1.7.a Directions: Write the correct form of the verb **to be** (**am, is** or **are**). The first one is done for you.

1. I ___am___ from Mexico.

2. You _____ from Mexico.

3. He _____ from Peru.

4. She _____ from Chicago.

5. We _____ from Paris.

6. You _____ from Guatemala.

7. They _____ from Texas.

8. Luis _____ from Cuba.

9. I _____ from Madrid.

10. Hector _____ from Cancun.

11. The teachers _____ from San Francisco.

12. Leo and Luis _____ from Nicaragua.

13. My mother _____ from Los Angeles.

14. You _____ from the United States.

15. Marco and Dan _____ from El Salvador.

16. I _____ from the Dominican Republic.

17. We _____ from Latin America.

18. My mother _____ from Canada.

19. They _____ from Mexico City.

20. You _____ from Zapopan.

1.7.b Directions: Translate these sentences. The first one is done for you. When you check your work, make sure that each of your sentences is exactly the same as the sentence in the Appendix in the back of this book.

1. Susan es de San Salvador.   Susan is from San Salvador. _____

2. Juan y Nancy son de Chicago.   _____

3. Mi hermana es de Dallas.   _____

4. Ellos son de Lima.   _____

5. Nosotros somos de San Juan.   _____

1.7.c Directions: One of the sentences in each pair is not a correct sentence. Cross out the **incorrect** sentence. The first one is done for you.

1a. She is from England.   1b. ~~She are from England.~~

2a. I are from New York.   2b. I am from New York.

3a. We is from Miami.   3b. We are from Miami.

4a. He is from Chicago.   4b. He are from Chicago.

5a. The boys are from Cuba.   5b. The boys am from Cuba.

6a. My from is Santiago.   6b. I am from Santiago.

7a. You is from Tokyo.   7b. You are from Tokyo.

8a. Lourdes are from the United States.   8b. Lourdes is from the United States.

This chart shows you the pattern of the sentences you have studied.

Subject (noun or pronoun)	Verb to be (ser o estar)	Location
I (Yo)	am (soy)	from La Paz. (de La Paz.)
Luis	is (es)	from Bogota. (de Bogotá.)
We (Nosotros, Nosotras)	are (somos)	from Caracas. (de Caracas.)

As you can see, each sentence begins with a noun or pronoun, followed by the conjugated form of the verb **to be**, followed by a location. While this may seem straightforward, it's very easy to make mistakes. Here are some examples of the kinds of mistakes new English speakers often make.

Sentences with no subject

In English, it is <u>not</u> correct to say

> ▶ ~~Is from Morelia.~~ (Es de Morelia.)

In English, unlike in Spanish, you can't omit the subject. (The only exception is commands, which aren't discussed in this book.) It is correct, for example, to say

> ▶ **Luis** is from Morelia. (Luis es de Morelia.)

Or you can say

> ▶ **He** is from Morelia. (Él es de Morelia.)

Sentences with a redundant subject

It is <u>not</u> correct to say

> ▶ ~~Luis he is from Morelia. (Luis, él es de Morelia.)~~

This sentence isn't correct because you can't use both a noun and a pronoun for the same subject. Instead, you can either say

> ▶ **Luis** is from Morelia. (Luis es de Morelia.)

Or you can say

> ▶ **He** is from Morelia. (Él es de Morelia.)

Sentences with no verb

Another common mistake is to omit the verb altogether. For example,

> ▶ ~~He from Morelia. (Él de Morelia.)~~

Note that, in English, a grammatically correct sentence <u>must</u> include a verb.

1.8.a Directions: Two sentences on each line are correct and one is incorrect. Cross out the **incorrect** sentence. The first one is done for you.

1a. ~~Susan she is from NY.~~   1b. She is from NY.   1c. Susan is from NY.

2a. Bob is from Boston.   2b. Bob he is from Boston. 2c. He is from Boston.

3a. Lily is from Reno.   3b. She is from Reno.   3c. Lily she is from Reno.

4a. He is from Peru.   4b. Dan he is from Peru.   4c. Dan is from Peru.

5a. The girls they are from LA. 5b. They are from LA.   5c. The girls are from LA.

1.8.b Directions: One sentence on each line is correct and one is incorrect. Cross out the **incorrect** sentence on each line. The first one is done for you.

1a. ~~Is from NY.~~   1b. She is from NY.

2a. Jose he is from Ecatepec.   2b. Jose is from Ecatepec.

3a. Are from Ciudad Juárez.   3b. Louisa and Anita are from Ciudad Juárez.

4a. Is from Puerto Rico.   4b. He is from Puerto Rico.

5a. Lisa she is from Camaguey.   5b. Lisa is from Camaguey.

6a. We are from San Luis Potosí.   6b. Are from San Luis Potosí.

7a. ~~I am NY.~~   7b. I am from NY.

8a. Ernesto is Guadalajara.   8b. Ernesto is from Guadalajara.

9a. Louisa and Anita from LA.   9b. Louisa and Anita are from LA.

10a. He is from Guatemala City.   10b. He is Guatemala City.

11a. Lisa from Culiacan.   11b. Lisa is from Culiacan.

12a. We are from Zapopan.   12b. We from Zapopan.

13a. I from Santo Domingo.   13b. I am from Santo Domingo.

14a. They are Guadalupe.   14b. They are from Guadalupe.

1.8.c Directions: Write the correct form of the verb **to be** (**am, is** or **are**). The first one is done for you.

1. I __am__ from Madrid.   5. They _____ from Australia.

2. You _____ from the Dominican Republic. 6. You _____ from Guatemala.

3. Antonio _____ from Bolivia.   7. The students _____ from Puerto Rico.

4. We _____ from Honduras.   8. Esmeralda _____ from the United States.

📖 *Chapter 1 Summary*

Nouns

► A *noun (sustantivo)* is a person, place, animal or thing.

► A noun can be *singular* or *plural.* A *singular noun (sustantivo singular)* refers to one noun (that is, one person, place, animal or thing.). A *plural noun (sustantivo plural)* refers to more than one noun. In both Spanish and English, you usually make a noun plural by adding an **s**.

Pronouns

► A *pronoun (pronombre)* is a word that you can use to replace a noun.

► In English, a *subject pronoun* or *personal pronoun (pronombre personal)* is a pronoun that takes the place of a noun that is the subject of the sentence.

► The English subject pronouns with Spanish translations are as follows:

Personal Pronouns	
I (yo)	**we** (nosotros, nosotras)
he (él)	**you** (tú, usted, ustedes)
she (ella)	**they** (ellos, ellas)
it	

Verbs

► A *verb (verbo)* is a word that shows action or state of being.

Subjects

► The *subject (sujeto)* of a sentence is the person or thing that the sentence is about.

The verb to be

► The most common English verb is **to be** (ser and estar). You conjugate the verb **to be** like this:

I am	**we** are
he is, **she** is	**you** are
it is	**they** are

The article the

► **The** means el, la, los and las.

English sentences

► English sentences always include a subject and a verb.

► The English sentences you learned in Chapter 1 have this form:

Subjeto (noun or pronoun)	Verb **to be** (ser o estar)	Location
I (Yo)	**am** (soy)	**from La Paz.** (de La Paz.)
Luis	**is** (eres)	**from Bogota.** (de Bogotá.)
We (Nosotros, Nosotras)	**are** (somos)	**from Caracas.** (de Caracas.)

 **More Practice!**

P1.a Directions: Make each noun plural. The first one is done for you.

1. son ____sons____   5. book _____

2. daugher _____   6. sister _____

3. friend _____   7. teacher _____

4. boy _____   8. girl _____

P1.b Directions: Write **S** after the noun if it is singular and **P** after the noun if it is plural. The first two are done for you.

1. dogs   P _____   9. books   _____

2. cat   S _____   10. girl   _____

3. store   _____   11. table   _____

4. stores   _____   12. cars   _____

5. chair   _____   13. dog   _____

6. car   _____   14. cats   _____

7. book   _____   15. house   _____

8. chairs   _____   16. teachers _____

P1.c Directions: Put one line under the subject of each sentence and two lines under the verb, ser or estar. The first one is done for you.

1. <u>Mi hermana</u> <u>está</u> feliz.   6. Nosotros estamos aquí.

2. Ellos son amigos.   7. La fiesta es en el parque.

3. El libro es de Benito.   8. Las mujeres son muy bonitas.

4. Ella está en su casa.   9. Él es de los Estados Unidos.

5. Enrique es el capitán.   10. Las maestras están en la oficina.

P1.d Directions: Translate these subject pronouns from Spanish to English. The first one is done for you.

1. ellos   they _____   6. él   _____

2. yo   _____   7. ustedes   _____

3. nosotras   _____   8. ellas   _____

4. usted   _____   9. nosotros   _____

5. ella   _____   10. tú   _____

P1.e Directions: Write the correct form of the verb **to be** (**am, is** or **are**). The first one is done for you.

1. He __is__ from Sinaloa.
2. We _____ from Nayarit.
3. Antonio _____ from Yucatan.
4. Lilia and Jose _____ from Guerrero.
5. They _____ from Campeche.
6. You _____ from Santo Domingo.
7. The brothers _____ from Tobasco.
8. Alejandro _____ from Guanajuato.
9. Obdula _____ from Colima.
10. Sara _____ from Havana.

11. I _____ from Mexico City.
12. The teacher _____ from Zacatecas.
13. The students _____ from the USA.
14. Mr. Lopez _____ from Coahuila.
15. I _____ from Quintana Roo.
16. My boyfriend (novio) _____ from Tamaulipas.
17. My girlfriend (novia) _____ from Hidalgo.
18. You _____ from Aguascalientes.
19. She _____ from Baja California Sur.
20. I _____ from Baja California Norte.

P1.f Directions: Change the subject in each sentence from singular to plural. Then change the verb to make a correct sentence. The first one is done for you.

1. The girl is from Mexico.   The girls are from Mexico.

2. The boy is from Puerto Rico. _____

3. The teacher is from Guatemala. _____

4. The girl is from Bolivia. _____

5. The doctor is from El Salvador. _____

6. The student is from San Francisco. _____

P1.g Directions: One sentence on each line is correct and one is incorrect. Crossout the **incorrect** sentence on each line.

1a. ~~I am Chicago.~~
2a. Ernesto is from Guadalajara.
3a. Louisa and Anita from LA.
4a. Is from Guatemala City.
5a. Lisa is from Haiti.
6a. We are from Caracas.
7a. I from Mexico City.
8a. Louisa she is from Guadalupe.
9a. He from the United States.
10a. My brother is from Boston.

1b. I am from Chicago.
2b. Ernesto he is from Guadalajara.
3b. Louisa and Anita are from LA.
4b. He is from Guatemala City.
5b. Lisa she is from Haiti.
6b. We from Caracas.
7b. I am from Mexico City.
8b. Louisa is from Guadalupe.
9b. He is from the United States.
10b. My brother he from Boston.

P1.h Directions: Rewrite the sentence by replacing the underlined words with a pronoun (**he, she** or **they**). The first one is done for you.

1. <u>The girls</u> are from New York.   They are from New York.

2. <u>The girl</u> is from Panama.

3. <u>My brothers</u> are from Brazil.

4. <u>My father</u> is from Argentina.

5. <u>The teachers</u> are from Santiago.

6. <u>Miguel and Carlos</u> are from Las Vegas.

7. <u>Martin</u> is from the United States.

8. <u>My mother</u> is from Mexico City.

P1.i Directions: Translate these sentences into English.

1. Ella es de Nicaragua.   She is from Nicaragua.

2. Nosotros somos de San Diego.

3. Las niñas son de Chicago.

4. La maestra es de Guadalajara.

5. Ellos son de Cancún.

6. Los estudiantes son de Bogotá.

7. Yo soy de San Francisco.

8. Los maestros son de Havana.

Chapter 2

I am a cook.

In this chapter you'll continue to build your knowledge of English by learning how to talk about your job. You'll also use adjectives like **tall** (alto) and **handsome** (guapo) to describe people you know.

At the end of the chapter you will know how to
- distinguish between **a** and **an**.
- tell people your occupation.
- use adjectives to describe people and objects.
- use the pronoun **it**.
- use demonstrative adjectives to identify the noun that you're referring to.

In chapter 1 you learned about the important word **the**. In this chapter you'll learn how to use **a** and **an** before singular nouns. Study these examples:

an apple
(una manzana)

a house
(una casa)

Grammar rule: To determine whether you use **a** or **an**, follow these rules:

▶ If a noun begins with a *vowel*, you use **an**. The vowels in English are **a, e, i, o** and **u**. You say **an apple** (una manzana) because **apple** begins with **a**, which is a *vowel*.

▶ If a noun begins with a *consonant*, you use **a** (A *consonant* is a letter which is not a vowel.) In English, the consonants are **b, c, d, f, g, h, j, k, l, m, n, p, q, r, s, t, v, w, x, y** and **z.** You say **a book** (un libro) because **book** begins with **b**, which is a consonant.

There is a reason for these rules. It is easier to pronounce **an apple** than to pronounce **a apple**.

Each of these nouns begins with a vowel, so they are preceded by **an**. Here are examples of how **an** is used:

an apple (una manzana)	**an egg** (un huevo)
an opera (una ópera)	**an artist** (un artista, una artista)

Each of these nouns begins with a consonant, so they are preceded by **a**. Here are examples of how **a** is used:

a book (un libro)	**a teacher** (un maestro, una maestra)
a boy (un niño)	**a girl** (una niña)

Grammar Summary

The words **a, an** and **the** are articles. You have now learned all the articles in the English language! Here they are:

▶ **the** (el, la, los, las)

▶ **a, an** (un, una)

2.1.a Directions: Write **V** next to each letter that is a vowel and **C** next to each letter that is a consonant.

1. a V	6. o ____	11. b ____	16. e ____
2. d C	7. q ____	12. w ____	17. n ____
3. g ____	8. s ____	13. i ____	18. p ____
4. j ____	9. u ____	14. c ____	19. k ____
5. m ____	10. t ____	15. f ____	20. l ____

2.1.b Directions: Write **a** or **an** before each of the singular nouns below.

1. _a_ book	6. ____ dog	11. ____ table	16. ____ teacher
2. ____ airplane	7. ____ egg	12. ____ doctor	17. ____ eraser
3. ____ apple	8. ____ store	13. ____ orange	18. ____ nurse
4. ____ girl	9. ____ artist	14. ____ car	19. ____ opera
5. ____ man	10. ____ cat	15. ____ chair	20. ____ school

2.1.c Directions: One of the phrases in each pair is not correct. Cross out the **incorrect** phrase.

1a. ~~a egg~~	1b. an egg
2a. a book	2b. an book
3a. a opera	3b. an opera
4a. a chair	4b. an chair
5a. a student	5b. an student
6a. a apple	6b. an apple

2.1.d Directions: Translate these phrases.

1. el gato _the cat_	9. las tiendas _____
2. un gato _____	10. la tienda _____
3. la casa _____	11. una tienda _____
4. una casa _____	12. la silla _____
5. un maestro _____	13. una niña _____
6. el maestro _____	14. la niña _____
7. los maestros _____	15. las niñas _____
8. los gatos _____	16. una silla _____

In this section, you'll learn to talk about your job. Read these conversations:

*¿Cuál es tu trabajo?
**Soy cocinero. Yo soy cocinera.

*¿Qué haces?
**Soy artista. Yo soy artista.

In Spanish you never use un or una before the name of a job. That's why you say

▶ Yo soy cocinero.

In English, you <u>must</u> include **a** or **an** before the name of a job when the subject of the sentence is singular.

▶ I am **a** cook.

Study this list of jobs. You'll use this vocabulary in the exercises on the next page.

Vocabulary: Jobs	
artist (artista)	**lawyer** (abogado, abogada)
cashier (cajero, cajera)	**nurse** (enfermero, enfermera)
construction worker (albañil)	**babysitter** (niñera)
cook (cocinero, cocinera)	**salesperson** (vendedor, vendedora)
homemaker (ama de casa)	**teacher** (maestro, maestra)
engineer (ingeniero, ingeniera)	**waiter** (mesero)
gardener (jardinero, jardinera)	**waitress** (mesera)

In English, the names of jobs do not change regardless of whether the person who does the job is a man or a woman. For example, a **teacher** can be a man or a woman. The same is true for **lawyer, doctor, cook** and so on. The one exception in this list is **waiter** and **waitress**. A **waiter** is almost always a man and a **waitress** is always a woman.

👁 **¡Cuidado!** You use **a** when you are talking about your job. You don't use **a** when you are talking about where you are from.

2.2.a Directions: Complete each sentence using **a** or **an**.

1. I am __a__ gardener.
2. She is _____ teacher.
3. Sam is _____ engineer.
4. Anna is _____ waitress.
5. Peter is _____ waiter.
6. Laura is _____ artist.
7. My (Mi) mother is _____ lawyer.
8. I am _____ doctor.

9. Armida is _____ cashier.
10. He is _____ construction worker.
11. Myra is _____ cook.
12. My sister is _____ homemaker.
13. Benito is _____ artist.
14. Eva is _____ salesperson.
15. Angi is _____ waitress.
16. My father is _____ waiter.

2.2.b Directions: Translate the following sentences. Remember you only need to use **a** or **an** before the name of the job.

1. Yo soy médico.   I am a doctor.
2. Anna es cajera.
3. Juan es maestro.
4. Mi hermano es mesero.
5. Juan es albañil.
6. Él es ingeniero.
7. María es de Cuba.
8. Lucas es vendedor.
9. Lily es vendedora.
10. Sandra es ama de casa.
11. Yo soy niñera.
12. Mi madre es ingeniera.

2.2.c Directions: One of the sentences in each pair is not a correct sentence. Cross out the **incorrect** sentence.

1a. I am a doctor.
2a. Anna is a artist.
3a. Caroline is a doctor.
4a. Marco is a engineer.
5a. Tom is from San Pablo.
6a. Laura is a nurse.

1b. ~~I am an doctor.~~
2b. Anna is an artist.
3b. Caroline is an doctor.
4b. Marco is an engineer.
5b. Tom is from a San Pablo.
6b. Laura is an nurse.

Talking About Other People's Jobs

In this section, we'll learn to talk about other people's jobs. Study these sentences:

*Mi hermana es médica.

*Mis hermanos son músicos.

In the first drawing, you must use the article **a** because the noun that follows is singular. In the second drawing, notice the following:

▶ **Musicians** is plural because you're talking about more than one musician.

▶ You don't need **a** or **an** here because the noun that follows, **musicians**, is plural.

Grammar Rule: You never use **a** or **an** before a plural noun.

This chart shows the pattern of sentences about jobs.

Subject (noun or pronoun)	Verb to be	a or an	Occupation
I	am	a	nurse.
María	is	an	engineer.
María and Jose	are		nurses.
They	are		engineers

This chart shows examples of correct sentences and incorrect sentences. Do you know why the sentences in the right column are incorrect?

Correct sentences	Incorrect sentences
They are waiters. (Ellos son meseros.)	~~They are a waiters.~~
Peter and Paul are waiters. (Peter y Paul son meseros.)	~~Peter and Paul are a waiters.~~

2.3.a Directions: One of the sentences in each pair is not a correct sentence. Cross out the **incorrect** sentence.

1a. They are waiters.   1b. ~~They are a waiters.~~

2a. Anna and Amy are artist.   2b. Anna and Amy are artists.

3a. Coco and Adam are teachers.   3b. Coco and Adam are teacher.

4a. They are a engineers.   4b. They are engineers.

5a. Tom is a nurse.   5b. Tom is nurse.

6a. Miguel and Anna are cooks.   6b. Miguel and Anna are cook.

7a. He is a engineer.   7b. He is an engineer.

8a. They are artists.   8b. They are a artists.

2.3.b Directions: Make the subject of each sentence plural. Then change the rest of the sentence so that it is correct.

1. He is a doctor.   They are doctors.

2. He is a student.   ....

3. She is a nurse.   ....

4. He is a teacher.   ....

5. The girl is a student.   The girls are students.

6. The boy is a student.   ....

7. The girl is an artist.   ....

8. The boy is an artist.   ....

2.3.c Directions: Translate the following sentences. Remember: If the subject is singular, you need to use **a** or **an** before the name of the job. If the subject is plural, you don't use **a** or **an** before the name of the job.

1. Ellos son ingenieros.   They are engineers.

2. Ellas son cajeras.   ....

3. Martín y (and) Amanda son artistas. ....

4. Mi hermana es mesera.   ....

5. Juana y Adam son cocineros.   ....

6. Soy cocinero.   ....

7. Louisa es artista.   ....

8. Luis es vendedor.   ....

9. Lily y Chelsea son enfermeras.   ....

10. Sandra y Ramón son estudiantes.   ....

An *adjective* is a word that modifies or describes a noun or pronoun. Examples of adjectives are inteligente, guapo, bonito, rojo, caliente and fuerte.

▶ La casa es **bonita**.

▶ Estoy **enferma**.

▶ Los niños son **traviesos**.

Before you learn how to use adjectives in sentences, take a few minutes to learn these adjectives. You use these adjectives to describe what people look like.

tall (alto, alta, altos, altas)   **thin** (delgado, delgada,   **beautiful*, pretty*** (bonito,
short (bajo, baja, bajos,   delgados, delgadas   bonita, bonitos, bonitas)
   bajas)   **heavy** (gordo, gorda,
                                          gordos, gordas)

***Pretty** and **beautiful** are used to describe women and **handsome** is used to describe men. The opposite of **pretty** and **beautiful** is **ugly** (feo, fea, feos y feas).

You use these adjectives to describe other aspects of people.

Vocabulary: More adjectives that describe people	
happy	feliz, felices
sad	triste, tristes
intelligent	inteligente, inteligentes
hardworking	trabajador, trabajadora, trabajadores, trabajadoras
lazy	flojo, floja, flojos, flojas
good	buen, bueno, buena, buenos, buenas
bad	mal, malo, mala, malos, malas
healthy	saludable, saludables
sick	enfermo, enferma, enfermos, enfermas
tired	cansado, cansada, cansados, cansadas
young	joven, jóvenes
old	viejo, vieja, viejos, viejas

2.4.a Directions: Translate each adjective into Spanish.

1. young _joven_   5. sad _____   9. old _____

2. heavy _____   6. beautiful _____   10. healthy _____

3. thin _____   7. ugly _____   11. sick _____

4. happy _____   8. young _____   12. tired _____

2.4.b Directions: Translate each adjective into English.

1. alto _tall_   5. delgado _____

2. bajo/chaparro _short_   6. gordos _____

3. joven _____   7. guapo _____

4. vieja _____   8. bonitas _____

2.4.c Directions: Write the opposite of each adjective.

1. good _bad_   9. healthy _____

2. hardworking _____ 10. happy _____

3. thin _____   11. short _____

4. ugly _____   12. handsome _____

5. heavy _____   13. bad _____

6. sad _____   14. lazy _____

7. tall _____   15. sick _____

8. beautiful _____   16. young _____

2.4.d Directions: Answer these questions using your new vocabulary.

1. Write three adjectives that describe you. _____ _____ _____ _____

2. Write three adjectives that describe your mother. _____ _____ _____

3. Write three adjectives that describe your best friend. _____ _____

_____

Now that you know some English adjectives, you're ready to start using them. But before you do, you need to understand some important differences about how adjectives are used in Spanish and in English.

In Spanish, the ending of an adjective changes depending on whether the noun it describes is masculine or feminine and whether it is singular or plural. When you're referring to a female, the adjective that describes her usually ends in **a**. For example:

► María está **cansad<u>a</u>**.

When you're referring to a male, the adjective that describes him usually ends in **o**. For example:

► Frank está **cansad<u>o</u>**.

When an adjective refers to two or more people or things, the adjective ends in **s.** For example:

► Frank y Ernesto están **cansados**.

► Anna y Emma están **cansadas**.

In English spelling adjectives is easy because the endings of the adjective never change. Read these sentences:

*María está cansada.   **Frank está cansado.*   **María y Frank están cansados.*

As you see, the adjective, **tired,** is spelled exactly the same way in each sentence.

This chart shows the pattern used in English sentences that include the verb **to be** plus an adjective.

Subject (noun or pronoun)	Verb **to be**	Adjective
I	am	tired.
Luis	is	tired.
The students	are	tired.

2.5.a Directions: Each line contains one correct sentence and one incorrect sentence. Cross out the **incorrect** sentence. (Remember that, in English, you never add **s** to adjectives.)

1a. ~~My sisters are sads.~~   1b. My sisters are sad.

2a. They are intelligent.   2b. They are intelligents.

3a. We are olds.   3b. We are old.

4a. The girls are beautiful.   4b. The girls are beautifuls.

5a. The dogs are uglys.   5b. The dogs are ugly.

6a. My father is young.   6b. My father is youngs.

2.5.b Directions: Make the subject of each sentence plural. Then change the verb so that the sentence is correct.

1. The girl is tired.   The girls are tired.

2. The teacher is happy.   The teachers are happy.

3. The doctor is handsome.   _____

4. The nurse is hardworking.   _____

5. The lawyer is intelligent.   _____

6. The waiter is young.   _____

7. The engineer is beautiful.   _____

8. The cook is thin.   _____

2.5.c Directions: Translate each sentence.

1. Martha es joven.   Martha is young.

2. Los estudiantes son inteligentes.   The students are intelligent.

3. Martín es gordo.   _____

4. Los jardineros están enfermos.   _____

5. Yo estoy cansada.   _____

6. La maestra es bonita.   _____

7. Los cajeros son flojos.   _____

8. Las niñeras están felices.   _____

9. Las abogadas son trabajadoras.   _____

10. Yo soy alta.   _____

11. Ernesto es viejo.   _____

12. Luis es joven.   _____

2.6   Using *It*

So far, all of the English sentences you have written have been about people. But suppose you want to talk about your house or your car or your job? The English subject pronoun that you use to talk about things and animals is **it**. This subject pronoun does not exist in Spanish. Read this conversation:

*¿Dónde está la llave? **Está en la mesa.

Notice that, in the Spanish translation of this sentence, there is no word for **it**. In English, the use of **it** is not optional! The following table gives examples of sentences that use **it** correctly and examples of sentences that fail to include **it**.

Correct sentences	Incorrect sentences
It is on the table. (Está en la mesa.)	~~Is on the the table.~~
My car is broken. **It** is old. (Mi carro está roto. Es viejo.)	My car is broken. ~~Is old.~~

When referring to animals, you can either use **it, he** or **she**. Many people use **he** or **she** to talk about a pet such as a dog or a cat, but use **it** to talk about animals that aren't part of their everyday lives.

Colors are adjectives too

One of the most common types of adjectives are colors. Study this table.

Vocabulary: Colors			
red	rojo, roja, rojos, rojas	**purple**	morado, morada, morados, moradas
yellow	amarillo, amarilla, amarillos, amarillas	**brown**	café, cafés, marrón, marrones
green	verde, verdes	**black**	negro, negra, negros, negras
blue	azul, azules	**white**	blanco, blanca, blancos, blancas
orange	naranja, naranjas, anaranjado, anaranjada, anaranjados, anaranjadas	**gray**	gris, grises

2.6.a Directions: Translate each color.

1. azul _blue_____

2. rojo _____

3. blanco _____

4. negro _____

5. naranja _____

6. morado _____

7. café _____

8. amarillo _____

9. verde _____

10. gris _____

2.6.b Directions: Write the pronoun—**it, he** or **she**—that you can substitute for each noun.

1. the book _it____

2. Mario _____

3. the table _____

4. Anna _____

5. the girl _____

6. the boy _____

7. the store _____

8. the house _____

9. Lucas _____

10. Beatrice _____

11. the chair _____

12. the egg _____

2.6.c Directions: Substitute the underlined words with the pronoun **it, he** or **she**.

1. The car is red.   It is red._____

2. The table is black and white.   _____

3. Anna is tired.   _____

4. The book is expensive (caro).   _____

5. The chair is blue.   _____

6. My father is tall.   _____

7. The car is green.   _____

8. Elizabeth is happy.   _____

9. The store is dirty (sucio).   _____

10. The dress (vestido) is yellow and purple. _____

2.6.d Directions: One of the sentences in each pair is not a correct sentence. Cross out the **incorrect** sentence.

1a. ~~Is big.~~

2a. It is a book.

3a. She is from New York.

4a. Is a doctor.

5a. Is a student.

6a. It is new.

1b. It is big.

2b. Is a book.

3b. Is from New York.

4b. He is a doctor.

5b. She is a student.

6b. Is new.

In the last section you learned that you use the pronoun **it** to refer to one object such as a book or chair. But suppose you want to refer to more than one object? To do that, you use the pronoun **they**, the same pronoun you use to refer to more than one person.

Here is an example of a sentence that uses the pronoun **they** to refer to more than one object.

> ► The dresses are new. **They** are beautiful. (Los vestidos son nuevos. Son bonitos.)

English vs. Spanish: In Spanish it is common to place commas at the end of short statements. In English, a period <u>must</u> go at the end of every statement.

The following table shows examples of sentences that use the pronouns **it** and **they** correctly and examples of incorrect sentences that fail to include them.

Correct sentences	Incorrect sentences
They are broken. (Están rotos.)	~~Are broken.~~
They are from Chicago. (Ellos son de Chicago.)	~~Are from Chicago.~~
It is new. (Es nuevo.)	~~Is new.~~

These drawings illustrate several common adjectives that you can use to describe objects around you.

small (pequeño, pequena, pequeños, pequeñas
big, large (gran, grande, grandes)

new (nuevo, nueva, nuevos, nuevas)
old (viejo, vieja, viejos, viejas)

cheap (barato, barata, baratos, baratas)
expensive (caro, cara, caros, caras)

Vocabulary: More adjectives	
broken	roto, rota, rotos, rotas
clean	limpio, limpia, limpios, limpias
dirty	sucio, sucia, sucios, sucias

2.7.a Directions: Write the opposite of each adjective.

1. old ___new___   6. happy _____
2. beautiful _____   7. tall _____
3. cheap _____   8. black _____
4. young _____   9. small _____
5. big _____   10. thin _____

2.7.b Directions: Write the pronoun—**it, he, she** or **they**—that you can substitute for each noun.

1. the book ___it___   6. the girls _____   11. the artists _____
2. the books _____   7. the stores _____   12. the dress _____
3. the table _____   8. the houses _____   13. Susan _____
4. the tables _____   9. the lawyers _____ 14. the chairs _____
5. the girl _____   10. Benjamin _____   15. the brothers _____

2.7.c Directions: Choose either **it** or **they**.

1. The chair is new. _____It_____ is yellow and (y) blue.
2. The chairs are new. _____ are yellow and blue.
3. The dress is from Guatemala. _____ is beautiful.
4. The dresses are from Italy. _____ are pretty.
5. The car is old. _____ is broken.
6. The houses are new. _____ are big.

2.7.d Directions: Translate these sentences. Check your work with the answers in Appendix A to make sure that every word is correct.

1. El libro es nuevo. Es interesante.   The book is new. It is interesting. _____
2. La casa es grande. Es bonita. _____
3. Los vestidos son caros. Son de París. _____
4. El carro es viejo. Está roto. _____
5. La silla es naranja. Es fea. _____

As you now know, an *adjective* is a word that modifies or describes a noun or pronoun. In English, a *demonstrative adjective* is an adjective that explains whether something or someone is near by or far away. Consider this sentence:

> ► **This** book is interesting. (**Este** libro es interesante.)

This (este) is a demonstrative adjective because it points out that the book being referred to is near by.

The following drawings illustrate the demonstrative adjectives.

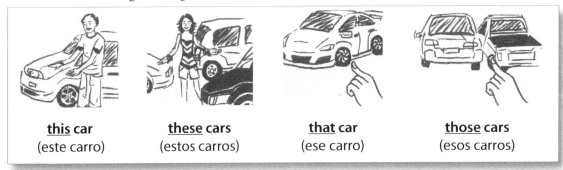

| **this** car | **these** cars | **that** car | **those** cars |
| (este carro) | (estos carros) | (ese carro) | (esos carros) |

Notice the following:

> ► You use **this** and **that** before singular nouns and you use **these** and **those** before plural nouns.

> ► You use **this** and **these** to refer to objects that are near you and **that** and **those** to refer to objects that are farther away from you.

> ► There are no demonstrative adjectives in English that you use in place of the Spanish demonstrative adjectives aquel, aquella, aquellos, aquellas, and aquello. Instead you simply say **over there**. For example, if you're pointing out a friend's new car on the other side of the parking lot you might say

> > **The car over there is new.** (Aquel carro es nuevo.)

This list introduces you to some vocabulary that's useful to students. You'll use these words in the next exercise.

Vocabulary: School supplies	
backpack (mochila)	**notebook** (cuaderno)
pencil (lápiz)	**textbook** (libro de texto)
eraser (borrador)	**dictionary** (diccionario)
pen (bolígrafo)	

2.8.a Directions: Look at the pictures. Then, complete the sentences with **this, that, these** or **those**.

1. ___This___ is my dictionary.

2. _____ are my pencils.

3. _____ is my pencil.

4. _____ is my eraser.

5. _____ are my notebooks.

6. ___That___ is my dog.

7. _____ is my sister.

8. _____ are my parents. *(padres)*

9. _____ is my grandmother. *(abuela)*

10. _____ are my relatives. *(parientes)*

2.8.b Directions: One of the sentences in each pair is not a correct sentence. Cross out the **incorrect** sentence.

1a. This dress is beautiful.

2a. This boy is my brother.

3a. These book is good.

4a. Those boys are from Laos.

5a. That girls are my daughter.

6a. These pencil is broken.

7a. That teacher is hardworking.

8a. Those textbooks are heavy.

1b. ~~These dress is beautiful~~.

2b. These boy is my brother.

3b. This book is good.

4b. That boys are from Laos.

5b. Those girls are my daughters.

6b. This pencil is broken.

7b. Those teacher is hardworking.

8b. That textbooks are heavy.

2.8.c. Directions: Translate these sentences.

1. Esta casa está limpia. This house is clean.

2. Estas casas son bonitas.

3. Esa tienda es grande.

4. Esas mesas están baratas.

5. Ese hombre es muy (very) alto.

6. Este diccionario es bueno.

7. Esas mochilas son caras

8. Este libro es interesante.

9. Esta mujer es maestra.

10. Estos niños son grandes.

You use the pronoun **we** (nosotros and nosotras) to refer to yourself and one or more people, either male or female. For example, if you are a woman talking about yourself and your best friend Angelica, you might say

▶ **We** are from Morelia. (Somos de Morelia. **Nosotras** somos de Morelia.)

If you are a man talking about yourself and your best friend Luis, you might also say

▶ **We** are from Morelia. (Somos de Morelia. **Nosotros** somos de Morelia.)

But sometimes, instead of using the pronoun **we,** you'll want to use specific names. For example,

▶ **Angelica and I** are from Morelia. (**Angélica y yo** somos de Morelia.)

There are several important things to notice about this sentence:

▶ You use the verb **are** because you are referring to more than one person.

▶ The pronoun **I** is capitalized even though it's not the first word in the sentence. The other subject pronouns (**you, he, she, it, we** and **they**) are only capitalized when they are the first word in the sentence.

▶ When referring to you and one or more people, the other people come first in the sentence. That is, you must begin the sentence with **Angelica**, and not with **I**.

Sentences with no subject

In English, it is not correct to say

▶ ~~Are from Morelia.~~ (Somos de Morelia.)

You can say

▶ **Luis and I** are from Morelia. (Luis y yo somos de Morelia.)

▶ **We** are from Morelia. (Somos de Morelia. Nosotros somos de Morelia.)

Sentences with subjects that repeat

It is not correct to say

▶ ~~Luis and I we are from Morelia. (Luis y yo nosotros somos de Morelia.)~~

This sentence isn't correct because you can't use both a noun and a pronoun for the same subject. You can either say

▶ **Luis and I** are from Morelia. (Luis y yo somos de Morelia.)

or

▶ **We** are from Morelia. (Somos de Morelia. Nosotros somos de Morelia.)

2.9.a Directions: Write the pronoun—**he, she, we** or **they**—that you can substitute for each noun.

1. Sam and I	we	11. Maria and Dale	
2. the boys		12. the doctors	
3. Lisa and I		13. the construction workers	
4. the girls and I		14. Bernardo and I	
5. the teachers		15. The girl	
6. the teacher and I		16. the doctor and I	
7. Caroline and Elliot		17. Marian and Phil	
8. Heidi and Ben		18. The babysitters	
9. Chelsea		19. The lawyer and the doctor	
10. Anna and I		20. My brother	

2.9.b Directions: Complete each sentence using **we** or **they**.

1. Susan and I are friends. ___We___ are from Mexico City.

2. The boys are construction workers. _____ are tired.

3. The dresses are from Guatemala. _____ are beautiful.

4. Anna and I are tired. _____ are teachers.

5. The cars are old. _____ are broken.

6. The houses are new. _____ are big.

7. Angi, Lucas and I are from London. _____ are engineers.

8. My sisters and I are homemakers. _____ are hardworking.

2.9.c Directions: One of the sentences in each pair is not a correct sentence. Cross out the **incorrect** sentence.

1a. ~~Bob and I we are from Reno.~~   1b. Bob and I are from Reno.

2a. Lisa and I are from Leon.   2b. Lisa and I we are from Leon.

3a. We from Seattle.   3b. We are from Seattle.

4a. We are doctors.   4b. We doctors.

5a. Are students.   5b. We are students.

6a. Sam and I we are tired.   6b. Sam and I are tired.

7a. I and Bruce are in love.   7b. Bruce and I are in love.

8a. Max and I are doctors.   8b. Max and I we are doctors.

A and **An:** **A** and **an** are used to refer to singular nouns.

► If the noun that follows begins with a ***vowel (vocal)***, you use **an**. The vowels in English are **a, e, i, o** and **u**. Example: **an apple**.

► If the noun that follows begins with a ***consonant (consonante)***, use **a**. (A consonant is any letter that is not a vowel. In English, the consonants are **b, c, d, f, g, h, j, k, l, m, n, p, q, r, s, t, v, w, x, y** and **z**.) Example: **a tree**.

► You <u>always</u> use **a** or **an** before occupations when the subject of the sentence is singular. You <u>never</u> use **a** or **an** before plural nouns.

Articles: Articles are words that often are placed before nouns. In English, the articles are **a, an** and **the**.

Articles	
a, an	un, una
the	el, la, los, las

Adjectives: An ***adjective (adjetivo)*** is a word that modifies or describes a noun or pronoun. Examples of adjectives are **big** (grande) and **blue** (azul). Unlike in Spanish, adjectives in English do not have endings.

Subject (noun or pronoun)	Verb to be	Adjective
I	am	<u>tired</u>.
Luis	is	<u>tired</u>.
We	are	<u>tired</u>.

It and **they:** Use the pronoun **it** to refer to a single thing or animal. Use the pronoun **they** to refer to more than one thing, animal or person. When talking about a new car, you'd say,

► **It** is new. (Es nuevo.)

When talking about more than one new car, you'd say

► **They** are new. (Son nuevos.)

We: Use the pronoun **we** in the same way that you use nosotros and nosotras in Spanish, that is, to refer to yourself and one or more other people.

► **We** are from New York. (Nosotros somos de Nueva York.)

To specifically refer to yourself and another person by name you say

► **Bernard and I** are from New York. (Bernard y yo somos de Nueva York.)

This, that, these and **those**

Demonstrative Pronouns	
this car (este carro)	**that** car (ese carro)
these cars (estos carros)	**those** cars (esos carros)

✍ More Practice!

P2.a Directions: Choose **a** or **an** before each of the singular nouns below.

1. _a_ chair	5. ___ artist	9. ___ engineer
2. ___ egg	6. ___ car	10. ___ job
3. ___ apple	7. ___ student	11. ___ nurse
4. ___ table	8. ___ orange	12. ___ opera

P2.b Directions: Complete each sentence using **a** or **an**.

1. I am _a_ teacher.
2. She is ___ cashier.
3. Sam is ___ engineer.
4. Anna is ___ artist.
5. Peter is ___ cook.
6. Laura is ___ artist.
7. My mother is ___ salesperson.

8. I am ___ engineer.
9. Alba is ___ babysitter.
10. He is ___ construction worker.
11. Francisco is ___ waiter.
12. Miguel is ___ cook.
13. Lucy is ___ homemaker.
14. Emma is ___ engineer.

P2.c Directions: One of the sentences in each pair is not a correct sentence. Cross out the **incorrect** sentence.

1a. That book is good.
2a. Bob and Al they are tired.
3a. Those pens are blue.
4a. Lucy and I are happy.
5a. These pens are new.
6a. The boys are at school.
7a. That boy he is tall.
8a. Max is teacher.
9a. They are tired.
10a. My sister she is beautiful.

1b. ~~These books is good.~~
2b. Bob and Al are tired.
3b. That pens are blue.
4b. Lucy and I we are happy.
5b. These pens is new.
6b. The boys they are at school.
7b. That boy is tall.
8b. Max is a teacher.
9b. They are tireds.
10b. My sister Is beautiful.

P2.d Directions: Write **N** if the word is a ***noun.*** Write **A** if the word is an ***adjetive.*** Remember: A ***noun*** is a person, place, animal or thing. An ***adjetive*** is a word that modifies or describes a noun.

1. beautiful	A	9. sad		17. houses	
2. doctor	N	10. house		18. boy	
3. chair		11. sick		19. chairs	
4. ugly		12. nurse		20. girls	
5. lazy		13. intelligent		21. healthy	
6. doctor		14. red		22. expensive	
7. dress		15. rice (arroz)		23. park (parque)	
8. thin		16. ball (pelota)		24. small	

P2.e Directions: Write the opposite of each adjective.

1. bad	good	8. sick	
2. cheap		9. old	
3. heavy		10. black	
4. handsome		11. lazy	
5. clean		12. short	
6. sad		13. happy	
7. tall		14. thin	

P2.f Directions: Rewrite the sentence by replacing the underlined words with a subject pronoun (**he, she, we, it** or **they**).

1. The table is new.   It is new.

2. The girl is tall.

3. The trees (los árboles) are beautiful.

4. The doctors are from Bolivia.

5. The chairs are blue and white.

6. The car is broken.

7. My sister and I are short.

8. The backpack is yellow.

9. Mario and Danny are tired.

10. My friends and I are hardworking.

11. The chair is purple.

12. The houses are small.

P2.g Directions: Write the correct form of the verb **to be** (**am, is** or **are**).

1. The student _is_ from Sinaloa.

2. We _____ intelligent.

3. Mario and I _____ construction workers.

4. The teachers _____ engineers.

5. That dress _____ purple.

6. It _____ expensive.

7. These dresses _____ new.

8. They _____ expensive.

9. Obdulia and I _____ from Loredo.

10. I _____ tall and thin.

11. Those girls and I _____ from Mexico City.

12. The cars _____ cheap.

P2.h Directions: The second sentence in each question is missing a word. Rewrite the **second** sentence so it is correct.

1. The car is blue. Is new.   _It is new._____

2. The cars are red. Are old.   _____

3. My sister is a student. Is intelligent.   _____

4. My boyfriend is a cook. Is nice.   _____

5. The chairs are new. Are expensive.   _____

P2.i Directions: Translate these sentences.

1. Susan y yo estamos cansadas.   _Susan and I are tired._____

2. Enrique y yo somos de Colombia.   _____

3. Ellas son enfermeras.   _____

4. Estos carros son nuevos.   _____

5. Lucy y yo somos trabajadores.   _____

6. Raúl es artista.   _____

7. Este diccionario es bueno.   _____

8. Estos estudiantes son inteligentes.   _____

9. Laura y yo somos de Argentina. Somos ingenieros.   _____

10. La silla y la mesa son nuevas. Son caras.   _____

11. Esos vestidos son bonitos. Son de París.   _____

12. María y Justin son de Sinaloa. Están enamorados.   _____

Chapter 3

Are you tired?

Conversation is a give-and-take process, with people taking turns asking and answering questions. In this chapter you'll continue to expand your understanding of English by learning how to ask and answer simple questions. By the end of the chapter, you'll be able to answer questions like "Are you tired?", "Are you married?", and even "Are you in love?".

At the end of the chapter you will know how to:
- use contractions.
- make negative sentences.
- ask and answer yes/no questions.

3.1   Using Contractions

A *contraction* is a word that is made by joining two other words. Read these conversations:

¿De dónde eres?
Soy de El México.

¿De dónde es Martin?
Él es de El Salvador.

¿De dónde es Minerva?
Ella es de Guatemala.

Notice that the contraction **I'm** combines the words **I** and **am** into a single word. The contraction **she's** is formed by combining **she** and **is** and the contraction **he's** is formed by combining **he** and **is**.

To make a contraction with a subject pronoun and the verb **to be**,

► Combine the pronoun (**I, you, he, she, it, we** or **they**) with the appropriate verb (**am, is** or **are**).

► Replace the first letter of the verb with an apostrophe (').

This table shows the contractions made with the verb **to be**.

Contractions with the verb to be

I + am	I'm	he + is	he's
you + are	you're	she + is	she's
we + are	we're	it + is	it's
they + are	they're		

You always make a contraction with an apostrophe, not a comma.

► ~~I,m tired.~~

Also, make sure that there isn't a space before the apostrophe. That's why the following sentence is incorrect.

► ~~I 'm tired.~~

3.1.a Directions: Write the contraction for each pair of words.

1. I am ___I'm___   3. He is _____   5. It is _____   7. They are _____

2. You are _____   4. She is _____   6. We are _____

3.1.b Directions: Rewrite each sentence using a contraction.

1. I am a babysitter.   I'm a babysitter.

2. She is from Brazil.   _____

3. It is expensive.   _____

4. They are healthy.   _____

5. He is my father.   _____

6. You are a nurse.   _____

7. I am lazy.   _____

8. We are old.   _____

3.1.c Directions: Complete each sentence with a contraction that combines a personal pronoun with **am, is** or **are**.

1. They're ____ from New York.   7. We _____ tired.

2. He _____ a doctor.   8. They _____ in Mexico.

3. We _____ students.   9. I _____ sad.

4. I _____ a nurse.   10. She _____ an engineer.

5. She _____ a student.   11. They _____ in Las Vegas.

6. It _____ good.   12. We _____ healthy.

3.1.d Directions: Translate these sentences. Use a contraction in every sentence.

1. Ella es delgada.   She's thin.

2. Él es ingeniero.   _____

3. Ellos son médicos.   _____

4. Yo soy floja.   _____

5. Ella es de Guadalajara.   _____

6. Ellas son gordas.   _____

Negative Sentences

In both English and Spanish, statements can either be **affirmative** or **negative**. This is an *affirmative* statement in Spanish:

▶ Él es de Nicaragua.

And this is a *negative* statement:

▶ Él **no** es de Nicaragua.

Notice that, in Spanish, negative statements usually include the word **no**.

Now look at these examples:

*Soy mesera.

*No soy mesero. Soy cocinero.

As you can see, the negative statement includes the word **not** immediately after the verb. Here are more examples:

Affirmative sentences	Negative sentences
I am tired. (Estoy cansado.)	**I am <u>not</u> tired.** (No estoy cansado.)
You are tired. (Estás cansado.)	**You are <u>not</u> tired.** (No estás cansado.)
Mario is tired. (Mario está cansado.) **He is tired.** (Él está cansado.)	**Mario is <u>not</u> tired.** (Mario no está cansado.) **He is <u>not</u> tired.** (Él no está cansado.)
Maria is tired. (María está cansada.) **She is tired.** (Ella está cansada.)	**Maria is <u>not</u> tired.** (María no está cansada.) **She is <u>not</u> tired.** (Ella no está cansada.)
The dog is tired. (El perro está cansado.) **It is tired.** (Está cansado.)	**The dog is <u>not</u> tired.** (El perro no está cansado.) **It is <u>not</u> tired.** (No está cansado.)
Maria and I are tired. (María y yo estamos cansados.) **We are tired.** (Nosotros estamos cansados.)	**Maria and I are <u>not</u> tired.** (María y yo no estamos cansados.) **We are <u>not</u> tired.** (Nosotros no estamos cansados.)
The girls are tired. (Las niñas están cansadas.)	**The girls are <u>not</u> tired.** (Las niñas no están cansadas.)
They are tired. (Ellas están cansadas.)	**They are <u>not</u> tired.** (Ellas no están cansadas.)

3.2.a Directions: Write **A** if the statement is affirmative and **N** if the statement is negative.

1. I am from New York.   A

2. I am not tired.   _____

3. Marian is tall.   _____

4. He is not short.   _____

5. The boys are lazy.   _____

6. The boys are not tired.   _____

7. The student is not hardworking.   _____

8. The car is yellow.   _____

9. Sandra and Eileen are not heavy.   _____

10. Angi and Peter are happy.   _____

3.2.b Directions: Make each affirmative statement negative.

1. I am happy.   I am not happy.

2. She is tired.   _____

3. We are from Los Angeles.   _____

4. They are students.   _____

5. Angi is a doctor.   _____

6. Barbara is beautiful.   _____

7. The table is new.   _____

8. My brother is from Japan.   _____

9. The nurses are sick.   _____

10. The girls are from the United States.   _____

11. The backpack is blue.   _____

12. The dresses are dirty.   _____

3.2.c Directions: Translate these sentences.

1. El carro no es nuevo.   The car is not new.

2. Ernesto no es de Lima.   _____

3. Los estudiantes no son trabajadores.   _____

4. Luis y yo no somos estudiantes.   _____

5. Angélica no es cajera. Es mesera.   Angelica is not a cashier. She is a waitress.

6. Daniel no es cajero. Es mesero.   _____

7. Marco no está enfermo. Está saludable.   _____

_____

8. Yo no soy de Nueva York. Soy de Houston.   _____

_____

You have learned that, in English, negative sentences with the verb **to be** include the word **not** instead of the word **no**. Here's the pattern:

Subject (noun or pronoun)	Verb to be	Not	Rest of sentence
I	am	not	from La Paz.
Luis	is	not	a doctor.
We	are	not	tired.

The rest of this section gives you examples of the kinds of mistakes new English speakers often make when speaking and writing negative sentences.

Negative statements that use no and omit the verb

Many people say,

  ▸ ~~I no tired.~~

This isn't a sentence because it doesn't include a verb. It also isn't correct because it uses **no** instead of **not**. The correct statement is

  ▸ I am not tired. (No estoy cansado.)

Negative statements that use no instead of not

Another common mistake is to remember the verb but still use **no**. For example

  ▸ ~~I am no tired. I no am tired.~~

The correct way to say this is

  ▸ I am not tired. (No estoy cansado.)

This chart shows correct and incorrect negative sentences. Do you know why the sentences in the right column are not correct?

Correct sentences	Incorrect sentences
She is not sick. (Ella no está enferma.)	~~She no sick.~~ ~~She no is sick.~~
Francisco is not lazy. (Francisco no es flojo.)	~~Francisco no lazy.~~ ~~Francisco no is lazy.~~
The car is not broken. (El carro no está roto.)	~~The car no is broken.~~ ~~The car is no broken.~~

3.3.a Directions: The following chart tells you the country and occupation of four people: Peter, Laura, Marco, and Monica. Read the chart. Then create true sentences by writing **is** or **is not** in the space provided below.

Name (Nombre)	Country (País)	Job (Trabajo/profesión)
Peter	El Salvador	salesperson
Laura	Cuba	lawyer
Marco	Mexico	construction worker
Monica	Nicaragua	nurse

1. Peter __is__ from El Salvador.

2. Peter __is not__ from Mexico.

3. Peter _____ a salesperson.

4. Peter _____ an engineer.

5. Laura _____ from El Salvador.

6. Laura _____ from Cuba.

7. Laura _____ a nurse.

8. Laura _____ a lawyer.

9. Marco _____ from Mexico.

10. Marco _____ from Nicaragua.

11. Marco _____ an engineer.

12. Marco _____ a construction worker.

13. Monica _____ from Nicaragua.

14. Monica _____ a nurse.

3.3.b Directions: One of the sentences in each pair is not a correct sentence. Cross out the **incorrect** sentence.

1a. ~~I no a doctor.~~

2a. She no is artist.

3a. Caroline is not heavy.

4a. Luis is not from Reno.

5a. Tom no is a student.

6a. They no are in love.

7a. We are not from Paris.

8a. She no is a artist.

1b. I am not a doctor.

2b. She is not an artist.

3b. Caroline no is heavy.

4b. Luis is no from Reno.

5b. Tom is not a student.

6b. They are not in love.

7b. We no from Paris.

8b. She is not an artist.

3.3.c Directions: Each sentence contains an error. Correct the sentence in the space provided. Each sentence should be negative.

1. I no tired. I am not tired.

2. Angi no from the U.S. _____

3. I no sick. _____

4. The girls no students. _____

5. The car no broken. _____

3.4   Contractions in Negative Sentences

Now that you know how to make negative sentences and how to make contractions, you're ready to use contractions in negative sentences.

Read the following sentence:

▶ She is not tired. (Ella no está cansada.)

To shorten the sentence with a contraction you can say

▶ She isn't tired. (Ella no está cansada.)

Grammar Recipe: To make a negative contraction with a sentence that includes **is** or **are**

▶ Combine **is** or **are** with the word **not**.

▶ Replace the **o** in **not** with an apostrophe (').

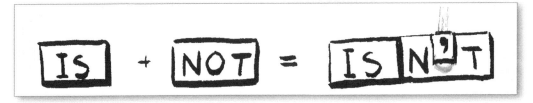

This chart shows examples of negative statements that don't use contractions and negative statements that use contractions. Additional contractions, such as **you're not, he's not** and so on, are included in Appendix B in the back of this book.

Negative sentences without contractions	Negative sentences with contractions	
I <u>am not</u> tired.	I'<u>m</u> not tired.	No estoy cansado.
You <u>are not</u> tired.	You <u>aren't</u> tired.	No estás cansado.
Juan <u>is not</u> tired. He <u>is not</u> tired.	Juan <u>isn't</u> tired. He <u>isn't</u> tired.	Juan no está cansado. Él no está cansado.
Lucy <u>is not</u> tired. She <u>is not</u> tired.	Lucy <u>isn't</u> tired. She <u>isn't</u> tired.	Lucy no está cansada. Ella no está cansada.
Luis and I <u>are not</u> tired. We <u>are not</u> tired.	Luis and I <u>aren't</u> tired. We <u>aren't</u> tired.	Luis y yo no estamos cansados. Nosotros no estamos cansados.
The students <u>are not</u> tired. They <u>are not</u> tired.	The students <u>aren't</u> tired. They <u>aren't</u> tired.	Los estudiantes no están cansados. Ellos no están cansados.

3.4.a Directions: Rewrite each sentence using a negative contraction.

1. I am not lazy. <u>I'm not lazy.</u>

2. You are not lazy. _____

3. He is not lazy. _____

4. She is not lazy. _____

5. We are not lazy. _____

6. They are not lazy. _____

7. It is not expensive. _____

8. The student is not from Tijuana. _____ _____

9. The book is not new. _____

10. I am not a homemaker. _____ _____

3.4.b Directions: Use negative contractions to complete these sentences.

1. The car is cheap. It <u>isn't</u> expensive.

2. I'm heavy. _____ not thin.

3. My mother is from Michoacan. She _____ from Sinaloa.

4. The students are lazy. They _____ hardworking.

5. Marvin and I are happy. We _____ sad.

6. My house is clean. It _____ dirty.

7. I'm a salesperson. _____ not a cashier.

8. My mother and father are old. They _____ young.

9. My boyfriend (novio) is handsome. He _____ ugly.

3.4.c Directions: Look at the chart below. Then write **is** or **isn't** to create true sentences.

Name (Nombre)	Type of animal (Tipo de animal)	Color
Dumbo	elephant (elefante)	gray
Donald	duck (pato)	yellow
Mickey	mouse (ratón)	black
Goofy	dog	black

1. Dumbo <u>isn't</u> a dog.

2. Dumbo <u>is</u> an elephant.

3. Dumbo _____ gray.

4. Donald _____ a duck.

5. Donald _____ a rabbit (conejo).

6. Donald _____ brown.

7. Mickey _____ a monkey.

8. Mickey _____ black.

9. Mickey _____ brown.

10. Goofy _____ a dog.

11. Goofy _____ a mouse.

12. Goofy _____ black.

3.5   Asking Yes/No Questions

Now that you know how to write affirmative and negative statements, you're ready to ask questions. But first, here are two important definitions:

A *statement* is a sentence that states something. An example of a statement is:

▶ I am in love. (Estoy enamorado.)

A *question* is a sentence that asks something. An example of a question is:

▶ Are you in love? (¿Estás enamorado?)

Punctuation rule: In English, a question has a question mark only at the end of a sentence.

In English, you almost always begin certain kinds of questions with a verb. For example,

▶ Is Mario from Mexico? (¿Es de México Mario? ¿Mario es de México?)

This kind of question is called a *yes/no question* because the answer is usually **yes** or **no**. Here's the pattern you use to ask yes/no questions that include the verb **to be**.

Verb to be	Subject (noun or pronoun)	Rest of sentence
Are	you	from New York?
Is	Lilia	a doctor?
Are	the students	tired?

The chart below shows more examples of the difference between statements and questions. Notice that

▶ A statement begins with a noun or pronoun followed by the verb **to be**. A statement ends with a period.

▶ A question begins with the verb **to be** followed by a noun or pronoun. A question ends with a question mark.

Statements	Questions	Statements	Questions
You are tired.	Are you tired?	Alma is tired.	Is Alma tired?
Marco is tired.	Is Marco tired?	She is tired.	Is she tired?

3.5.a Directions: Put either a period or a question mark in the space provided. Then write **Q** if the sentence is question and **S** if the sentence is a statement.

	Punctuation	Is this sentence a statement or a question?
1. Are you a student	a. _?_	b. _Q_
2. I am tired	a. _____	b. _____
3. Are you from New York	a. _____	b. _____
4. Are you in love	a. _____	b. _____
5. I am a doctor	a. _____	b. _____
6. Is Susan sick	a. _____	b. _____
7. Are you a doctor	a. _____	b. _____
8. Amanda is a housewife	a. _____	b. _____

3.5.b Directions: Write the verb necessary to complete each question.

1. _Are_ you from Spain?	10. _____ you from Seattle?
2. _____ you a teacher?	11. _____ the teachers tired?
3. _____ Juan from Mexico?	12. _____ the student hardworking?
4. _____ Martha intelligent?	13. _____ the housecleaners from Peru?
5. _____ he a lawyer?	14. _____ the boys from San Miguel?
6. _____ he from Spain?	15. _____ the girl from San Antonio?
7. _____ they hardworking?	16. _____ he at home (en casa)?
8. _____ she a nurse?	17. _____ Lydia at home?
9. _____ the nurses from Madrid?	18. _____ the boys happy?

3.5.c Directions: Put the words on each line in the correct order so that they create a question. Don't forget to start each question with a capital letter and end each question with a question mark.

1. she / is / tired /   _Is_   _she_   _tired?_

2. he / is / happy /   _____   _____   _____

3. they / are / doctors   _____   _____   _____

4. is / good / the / book   _____   _____   _____   _____

5. is / an / engineer / Lourdes   _____   _____   _____   _____

6. we / are / late (tarde)   _____   _____   _____

7. you / are / a / waitress   _____   _____   _____

8. they /are / lawyers   _____   _____   _____

Now that you know about asking questions, it's time to learn to answer them! Study these two conversations between a husband and a wife.

*¿Estás enferma?
**Sí.

*¿Estás enferma?
**No. Estoy cansada.

Notice that there aren't complete Spanish translations for the responses to the questions. That's because, in Spanish, you usually answer these question with a simple **sí** or **no**.

You can use a contraction in a negative short answer but not in an affirmative short answer. Thus it is correct to say,

▸ No, I'm not.

It is <u>not</u> correct to say

▸ ~~Yes, I'm.~~

You must say

▸ Yes, I am.

Capitalization and punctuation rules

When **yes** and **no** are the first word of a sentence, it is followed by a comma.

    Yes, she is.

▸ The only time you use a capital after the comma is if the word after the comma is **I** or a proper noun such as the name of a person or a country. Thus, these sentences have correct punctuation:

    Yes, I am.

    Yes, Laura is.

    Yes, she is.

The following sentence is incorrect.   Do you know why?

    ~~Yes, She is.~~

3.6.a Directions: Answer each question. Make sure to tell the truth! Use **Yes, I am.** or **No, I'm not.**

1. Are you from China?   No, I'm not.

2. Are you from Mexico?

3. Are you from Guatemala?

4. Are you hardworking?

5. Are you intelligent?

6. Are you lazy?

7. Are you tired?

8. Are you in love? (enamorado, enamorada)

9. Are you married? (casado, casada)

10. Are you single? (soltero, soltera)

3.6.b Directions: One of the answers to each question is not correct. Cross out the **incorrect** answer. Your answers don't have to be true.

1. Are you from Guadalajara?	a. ~~Yes, I'm.~~	b. Yes, I am.
2. Are you from Ecatepec?	a. Yes, I am.	b. Yes, I'm.
3. Are you from Mexico City?	a. No, I not.	b. No, I'm not.
4. Are you from Guatemala City?	a. No, I'm not.	b. No, I no.
5. Are you from Mexico?	a. Yes, I,am.	b. Yes, I am.
6. Are you tired?	a. No, I not.	b. No, I'm not.
7. Are you in love?	a. Yes, I am.	b. Yes, am.
8. Are you lazy?	a. No, I'm not.	b. No, I no.
9. Are you thin?	a. Yes, I'm.	b. Yes, I am.
10. Are you happy?	a. No, I'm not.	b. No I'm not

More Practice Answering Questions

You now know how to answer questions about yourself. But suppose you want to answer questions about other people? Study this table. Notice that there aren't complete Spanish translations for the responses to the questions. That's because, in Spanish, you usually answer the question with a simple **sí** or **no**.

Yes/No questions and answers in English	Yes/No questions and answers in Spanish
Are you tired? Yes, I am. No, I am not. No, I'm not.	¿Estás cansado? Sí. No.
Is Peter tired? Is he tired? Yes, he is. No, he is not. No, he isn't.	¿Está cansado Peter? ¿Está cansado él? Sí. No.
Is Anna tired? Is she tired? Yes, she is. No, she is not. No, she isn't.	¿Está cansada Anna? ¿Está cansada ella? Sí. No.
Are Laura and I tired? Are we tired? Yes, we are. No, we are not. No, we aren't.	¿Estamos cansados Laura y yo? ¿Estamos cansados nosotros? Sí. No.
Are the boys tired? Are they tired? Yes, they are. No, they are not. No, they aren't.	¿Están cansados los niños? ¿Están cansados ellos? Sí. No.
Is the car new? Is it new? Yes, it is. No, it is not. No, it isn't.	¿Es nuevo el carro? ¿Es nuevo? Sí. No.
Are the cars new? Are they new? Yes, they are. No, they are not. No, they aren't.	¿Son nuevos los carros? ¿Son nuevos? Sí. No.

Notice that you can use contractions in negative short answers but not in affirmative ones. Thus it is correct to say

► No, she isn't.

But it is not correct to say

► ~~Yes, she's.~~

3.7.a Directions: Look at the chart below. Then write **is** or **isn't** to create true statements.

Name	Marital status	Job
Manuel	*single (soltero)*	*waiter*
Anna	*married (casada)*	*doctor*
Sam	*divorced (divorciado)*	*engineer*
Lisa	*single*	*salesperson*

1. Is Manuel single?   Yes, he is.

2. Is Manuel a lawyer?   No, he isn't.

3. Is Anna married?

4. Is Anna a nurse?

5. Is Sam divorced?

6. Is Sam a doctor?

7. Is Lisa married?

8. Is Lisa a salesperson?

3.7.b Directions: Read the paragraph below. Then answer the questions with **Yes, she is.** or **No, she isn't.**

Anna Lopez is from Puebla, Mexico. She is short and thin. She is a cashier. She is hardworking. She is very (muy) happy because (porque) she is in love (enamorada).

1. Is Anna from Puebla, Mexico?   Yes, she is.

2. Is Anna tall?

3. Is Anna hardworking?

4. Is Anna an engineer?

5. Is Anna in love?

3.7.c Directions: One of the two responses to each question is grammatically incorrect. Cross out the **incorrect** response.

1. Are you from Mexico?	a. ~~Yes, I'm.~~	b. Yes, I am.
2. Is the car new?	a. Yes, it is.	b. Yes it is.
3. Are the children tired?	a. Yes, they are.	b. Yes, she is.
4. Are the friends happy?	a. Yes, he is.	b. Yes, they are.
5. Is Maria tired?	a. Yes, she is.	b. Yes, she's.
6. Are you at work?	a. No, she isn't.	b. No, I'm not.
7. Is the book interesting?	a. Yes, it is.	b. Yes, I am.
8. Is that store expensive?	a. No, I'm not.	b. No, it isn't.
9. Are the dresses new?	a. No, it isn't.	b. No, they aren't.

Negative Sentences

To make a sentence negative that includes the verb **to be**, place **not** immediately after the verb.

- ▶ Affirmative sentence: I am tired.
- ▶ Negative sentence: I am **not** tired.

Contractions

Contractions (contracciones) are words that are made by joining two words. To make a contraction with a pronoun and the verb **to be**

- ▶ Combine the pronoun (**I, you, he, she, it, we** or **they**) with the appropriate verb (**am, is** or **are**).
- ▶ Replace the first letter of the verb with an apostrophe (').

To make a negative contraction with the verb **to be** (**is** or **are**),

- ▶ Combine the appropriate verb (**is** or **are**) with the word **not**
- ▶ Replace the **o** in the word **not** with an apostrophe (').

The negative contraction for **I am not** doesn't follow this rule. It's simply **I'm not**.

Affirmative contractions		Negative contractions	
I + am	I'm	I am not	I'm not
you + are	you're	you are not	you aren't
he + is	he's	he is not	he isn't
she + is	she's	she is not	she isn't
it + is	it's	it is not	it isn't
we + are	we're	we are not	we aren't
they + are	they're	they are not	they aren't

Asking and answering yes/no questions

To create a yes/no question with the verb **to be**, reverse the subject and the verb:

- ▶ *Statement:* Maria is from Nicaragua.
- ▶ *Question:* Is Maria from Nicaragua?

This table illustrates how to answer yes/no questions that include the verb **to be**:

Are you tired?	Is Peter tired?	Is Anna tired?	Are the girls tired?	Is the table new?
Yes, I am.	Yes, he is.	Yes, she is.	Yes, they are.	Yes, it is.
No, I am not.	No, he is not.	No, she is not.	No, they are not.	No, it is not.
No, I'm not.	No, he isn't.	No, she isn't.	No, they aren't.	No, it isn't.

 **More Practice!**

P3.a Directions: Write the contraction for each pair of words.

1. he is ___he's___

2. you are _____

3. she is _____

4. we are _____

5. they are _____

6. it is _____

7. I am _____

P3.b Directions: Rewrite each sentence by replacing the underlined words with a contraction.

1. <u>I am</u> in love.   I'm in love.

2. <u>She is</u> from Mazatlan. _____

3. <u>We are</u> tired. _____

4. <u>She is</u> from Chile. _____

5. <u>They are</u> nurses. _____

6. <u>It is</u> yellow. _____

7. <u>They are</u> broken. _____

8. <u>They are</u> sick. _____

9. <u>We are</u> in love. _____

10. <u>He is</u> short. _____

P3.c Directions: Rewrite the phrase using a negative contraction.

1. he is not ___he isn't___

2. you are not _____

3. she is not _____

4. we are not _____

5. they are not _____

6. it is not _____

7. I am not _____

P3.d Directions: One of the sentences in each pair is not a correct sentence. Cross out the **incorrect** sentence.

1a. ~~I no a waitress.~~

2a. She isn't from San Diego.

3a. Ramon isn't sick.

4a. Yes, I am.

5a. Tom no is in love.

6a. They is not from Texas.

7a. Luis isn't happy.

8a. He no is a artist.

1b. I am not a waitress.

2b. She isn,t from San Diego.

3b. Ramon isn 't sick.

4b. Yes, I'm.

5b. Tom is not in love.

6b. They are not from Texas.

7b. Luis no is happy.

8b. He is not an artist.

P3.e Directions: Write the verb necessary to complete each question. Then, complete the answer using a contraction.

Question	Answer
1a. <u>Are</u> you from Spain?	1b. No, <u>I'm not.</u>
2a. _____ you a teacher?	2b. No, _____
3a. _____ Juan from Mexico?	3b. No, _____
4a. _____ Martha intelligent?	4b. No, _____
5a. _____ he a lawyer?	5b. No, _____
6a. _____ the car new?	6b. No, _____
7a. _____ tables old?	7b. No, _____
8a. _____ the dress expensive?	8b. No, _____

P3.f Directions: Make each sentence negative. In the first sentence, don't use a contraction. In the second sentence, use a contraction.

Affirmative sentence	Negative sentence <u>without</u> a contraction	Negative sentence <u>with</u> a contraction
I am from New York.	1a. <u>I am not from New York.</u>	1b. <u>I'm not from New York.</u>
She is tired.	2a. _____	2b. _____
Adam is a gardener.	3a. _____	3b. _____
The car is dirty.	4a. _____	4b. _____
We are happy.	5a. _____	5b. _____
The chairs are new.	6a. _____	6b. _____

P3.g Directions: Read the paragraph below. Then answer the questions with one of the following:

Yes, he is.	No, he isn't.
Yes, she is.	No, she isn't.
Yes, they are.	No, they aren't.

John is from Mexico. Anna is from Guatemala. They are married. They are in love. John is a waiter. He is tall and heavy. Anna is a nurse. She is tall and thin. They have (tienen) a dog. The dog is black and white. He is happy and lazy.

1. Is John from Mexico?   Yes, he is.

2. Is Anna from Mexico?   _____

3. Is Anna single?   _____

4. Are John and Anna married?   _____

5. Are John and Anna in love?   _____

6. Is John a cashier?   _____

7. Is John tall?   _____

8. Is Anna a nurse?   _____

9. Is Anna tall and thin?   _____

10. Is the dog brown?   _____

P3.h Directions: Put the words on each line in the correct order so that they create a <u>statement</u>. Don't forget to start each sentence with a capital letter and end it with a period.

1. he / sick / is /   He   is   sick.

2. they / young / are /

3. they / babysitters / are

4. from / are / they / Jalisco

5. Juana / hardworking / is

6. they / from / are / Buenos Aires

7. he / a / is / gardener

8. lawyers / they / are

P3.i Directions: Put the words on each line in the correct order so that they ask a <u>question</u>. Don't forget to start each question with a capital letter and end it with a question mark.

1. he / is / happy /   Is   he   happy?

2. they / are / happy /

3. they / are / gardeners

4. The boys / are / from / Jalisco

5. Lourdes / is / nurse / a

6. they / from / El Salvador / are

7. he / waiter / is / a

8. they / lawyers / are

P3.j Directions: Translate each sentence. <u>Use a contraction in every sentence.</u>

1. Él es mesero.   He's a waiter.

2. Angela no es mesera.

3. Daniela no es gorda.

4. Ellos son de Santa Fe.

5. Él es inteligente.

6. Yo estoy enferma.

7. José y yo no somos de Canadá.

8. La mesa no es morada.

9. Nosotras no somos amigas.

10. Ellos están cansados.

11. Yo no soy de Michoacán.

12. El carro no es barato.

Chapter 4

I have two brothers.

In everyday conversation, you'll often use the verb tener (**to have**) to talk about your family, your job and your appearance. In this chapter you'll learn to use this important verb.

At the end of this chapter you will be able to

- use the verb **to have** (tener).
- use irregular plural nouns like **men**, (hombres) **women** (mujeres), and **children** (niños).
- describe what you look like.
- count from one to one hundred.
- tell people your age.

You have already learned about **to be**, the most common verb in the English language. Now it's time to learn about another important verb, **to have** (tener). The following table shows you how to use this verb.

When to use **have**		When to use **has**	
I have	yo tengo	**he has**	él tiene
you have	tú tienes usted tiene	**she has**	ella tiene
we have	nosotros tenemos nosotras tenemos	**it has***	
they have	ellos tienen ellas tienen		

*As you know, there is no direct translation for **it** in Spanish.

Notice that the form of the verb that you use depends on the pronoun that precedes it.

- ► Use **have** after the pronouns **I, you, we** and **they** or any noun or phrase that pertains to that category.

- ► Use **has** after the pronouns **he, she** and **it**, or any noun or phrase that pertains to that category.

You use **have** in English in much the same way that you use tener in Spanish.

- ► I have a dog. (Tengo un perro.)

- ► She has a job. (Ella tiene un trabajo.)

- ► Andrew has a car. (Andrew tiene un carro.)

Notice that, in the first two Spanish sentences, you don't need to include a subject pronouns (yo and nosotros) because the ending on the verb tells you what pronoun you're talking about. In English you must include a pronoun before the verb.

You'll often use **have** and **has** to talk about how many of something you have, so study this table.

Vocabulary: Numbers from 1 to 10		
1. one ✱	6. six ✱✱✱✱✱✱
2. two ✱✱	7. seven ✱✱✱✱✱✱✱
3. three ✱✱✱	8. eight ✱✱✱✱✱✱✱✱
4. four ✱✱✱✱	9. nine ✱✱✱✱✱✱✱✱✱
5. five ✱✱✱✱✱	10. ten ✱✱✱✱✱✱✱✱✱✱

4.1.a Directions: Complete the phrases using **have** or **has**.

1. I ___have___
2. You _____
3. He _____
4. She _____
5. It _____
6. We _____
7. They _____
8. My friend and I _____
9. My aunt and my sister _____

10. Nancy _____
11. The homemakers _____
12. Peter _____
13. Bob and Tom _____
14. The boys _____
15. You and I _____
16. The students _____
17. The nurse _____
18. Roberto and I _____

4.1.b Directions: Write the correct number after the numeral.

1. 6 ___six___
2. 3 _____
3. 5 _____
4. 8 _____
5. 2 _____

6. 1 _____
7. 4 _____
8. 7 _____
9. 10 _____
10. 9 _____

4.1.c Directions: Complete each sentence using **have** or **has**.

1. I ___have___ a desk (escritorio.)
2. Andrew _____ two cars.
3. Linda _____ a backpack.
4. We _____ four books.
5. Marco and Lisa _____ a baby.
6. My sister _____ three dogs.
7. The teachers _____ books.
8. My mother and I _____ a house.
9. She _____ books.

10. They _____ friends.
11. I _____ a problem (problema).
12. Adam and Luisa _____ two children.
13. The student _____ a backpack.
14. The students _____ a class (una clase) at 9:00.
15. The house _____ a garden (jardín).
16. Andrew _____ a good teacher.
17. You _____ a large house.
18. The construction worker _____ a dog.

Using *Have* and *Has* with Singular and Plural Nouns

Now that you've learned about the verb **to have**, you're ready to learn more about using it.

Read these sentences:

- ► Susan has **a** book. (Susan tiene un libro.)
- ► Susan has **an** apple. (Susan tiene una manzana.)
- ► Susan has oranges. (Susan tiene naranjas.)

Do you remember why you use **a** in the first sentence, **an** in the second, and neither **a** nor **an** in the third? If not, read the Grammar Review below.

Grammar Review:

- ► If the noun that you are referring to begins with a *vowel,* you use **an**. The vowels in English are **a, e, i, o** and **u**. You say **an apple** (una manzana) because **apple** starts with **a**, which is a vowel.

- ► If the noun that you are referring to begins with a *consonant,* you use **a**. (A *consonant* is a letter which is not a vowel.) In English, the consonants are **b, c, d, f, g, h, j, k, m, n, p, q, r, s, t, v, w, x, y** and **z**. You say **a tree** (un árbol) because **tree** starts with **t**, which is a consonant.

- ► You <u>never</u> use **a** or **an** before a plural noun.

The following table shows examples of the correct and incorrect use of **a** and **an**.

Correct sentences	Incorrect sentences
I have apples in my backpack. (Tengo manzanas en mi mochila.)	~~I have a apples in my backpack.~~
I have an apple in my backpack. (Tengo una manzana en mi mochila.)	~~I have apple in my backpack.~~
I am an engineer. (Soy ingeniero.)	~~I am engineer.~~
We are engineers. (Somos ingenieros.)	~~We are engineer.~~ ~~We are an engineers.~~

4.2.a Directions: Look at the picture. Then write five sentences about what Hector has in this backpack.

1. He has four pencils.

2.

3.

4.

5.

4.2.b Directions: Complete each sentence using **have** or **has** and **a** or **an**.

1. I _have_ _a_ book.

2. Marcos _has_ _an_ orange.

3. My sister _____ _____ house in Paris.

4. The gardener _____ _____ job.

5. My friend _____ _____ apple.

6. I _____ _____ egg.

7. The students _____ _____ young teacher.

8. The boy _____ _____ backpack.

4.2.c Directions: One of the sentences in each pair is not a correct sentence. Cross out the **incorrect** sentence.

1a. I have a car.

2a. María has a books.

3a. I have orange.

4a. We have a teacher.

5a. Leo has four eraser.

6a. Laura has an egg.

7a. I have a problem.

8a. Lisa has two jobs.

9a. The boys have a bicycle.

10a. We have friend in Chicago.

1b. ~~I have car.~~

2b. María has books.

3b. I have an orange.

4b. We have teacher.

5b. Leo has four erasers.

6b. Laura has a egg.

7b. I have problem.

8b. Lisa has two job.

9b. The boys have bicycle.

10b. We have a friend in Chicago.

4.2.d Directions: Translate these sentences.

1. Tengo tres gatos. I have three cats.

2. Tengo tres lápices.

3. Laura tiene una mochila.

4. Sam tiene dos trabajos.

5. El estudiante tiene cuatro libros de texto.

6. Él tiene una hermana y cinco hermanos.

In Chapter 1, you learned that in English, as in Spanish, you make a singular noun plural by adding an **s**. This rule applies most of the time. There are, however, some important exceptions. This section explains some of them.

Rules for plural nouns: *dresses* and *churches*

Consider the word **dress** (vestido). The plural of **dress** is not ~~**dresss**~~, it's **dresses**. How do you know when you need to add **es** instead of **s**? Here's the rule:

Grammar rule: If a noun ends in **s, ss, sh, ch,** or **x**, add **es** to make it plural. For example, the plural of **church** (iglesia) is **churches** (iglesias). You add **es** because **church** ends in **ch**. Here are more examples:

- pea**ch**, peach**es** (durazno, duraznos)
- cla**ss**, class**es** (clase, clases)
- ki**ss**, kiss**es** (beso, besos)
- bo**x**, box**es** (caja, cajas)

More rules for plural nouns: *babies* and *cities*

Consider the word **baby** (bebé). The plural of **baby** is **babies**, not ~~**babys**~~.

Grammar rule: If a nouns ends in **y** proceded by a consonant, drop the **y** and add **ies** to make it plural.

Consider the word **city** (ciudad). The word ends in **y** preceded by a consonante, **t**. To make **city** plural, drop the **y** and add **ies**. The result is **cities**. Here are more examples:

- cher**ry**, cher**ries** (cereza, cerezas)
- par**ty**, par**ties** (fiesta, fiestas)
- la**dy**, la**dies** (dama, damas)

If a noun ends in **y** preceded by a vowel, you simply add **s** to make it plural. For example

- bo**y**, boy**s** (niño, niños)
- to**y**, toy**s** (juguete, juguetes)
- ke**y**, key**s** (llave, llaves)

4.3.a Directions: Make each singular noun plural.

1. cherry _cherries_
2. box _____
3. party _____
4. city _____
5. class _____
6. friend _____
7. church _____
8. store _____
9. dress _____
10. cat _____

11. kiss _____
12. boy _____
13. peach _____
14. baby _____
15. chair _____
16. toy _____
17. lady _____
18. nurse _____
19. sister _____
20. watch (reloj) _____

4.3.b Directions: Underline the correct verb in each sentence.

1. Angela (have, has) four dresses.
2. The cherries (is, are) good.
3. The church (is, are) big.
4. The school (have, has) ten classrooms (aulas).
5. The school (is, are) large.

6. Dulce (have, has) a baby.
7. Andrew (have, has) a toy.
8. The baby (is, are) beautiful.
9. The classes (is, are) interesting.
10. The boxes (is, are) heavy.

4.3.c. Directions: Translate these sentences.

1. Las cajas son pesadas.   The boxes are heavy.
2. Él tiene tres hermanas. _____
3. Esas naranjas son grandes. _____
4. Las iglesias son bonitas. _____
5. Ella tiene dos bebés. _____
6. Estos juguetes están rotos. _____
7. Los duraznos están malos. _____
8. Lillian tiene las llaves. _____

All of the nouns you have learned about thus far end in **s**. But there are a few plural nouns that do not end in **s**. These nouns are called *irregular plural nouns*. You'll learn about them in this section.

The following drawings illustrate the most common irregular plural nouns:

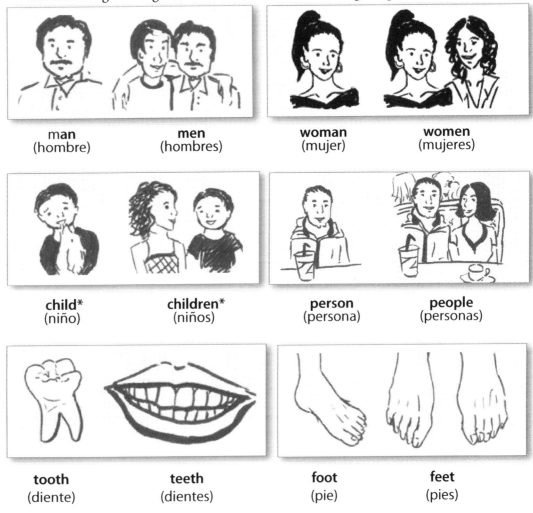

man
(hombre)

men
(hombres)

woman
(mujer)

women
(mujeres)

child*
(niño)

children*
(niños)

person
(persona)

people
(personas)

tooth
(diente)

teeth
(dientes)

foot
(pie)

feet
(pies)

Spanish vs. English. The English word for niño, **child**, refers either to a male or a female. Similarly, **children** (niños) refers to more than one child, whether those children are males, females, or a group of males and females. To refer to a single male child, you use the word **boy**. To refer to a single female child you use the word **girl**.

4.4.a Directions: Write the plural form of each singular noun.

1. man ___men___
2. person _____
3. tooth _____
4. child _____
5. foot _____
6. woman _____

4.4.b Directions: Write the singular form of each irregular plural noun.

1. people ___person___
2. teeth _____
3. women _____
4. men _____
5. feet _____
6. children _____

4.4.c Directions: Translate each phrase.

1. el niño ___the child___
2. un hombre ___a man___
3. el hombre _____
4. los hombres _____
5. los dientes _____
6. el diente _____
7. las personas _____
8. la persona _____
9. una persona _____
10. las mujeres _____
11. la mujer _____
12. una mujer _____

4.4.d Directions: Underline the correct word in each sentence.

1. I have two (child, <u>children</u>).
2. The (child, children) isn't sick.
3. The (woman, women) has two jobs.
4. That (man, men) has black eyes and black hair.
5. That (woman, women) is in love.
6. The (person, people) are in New York.
7. The (woman, women) has three dresses.
8. The (child, children) have four dogs.
9. My (foot, feet) are dirty.
10. The (man, men) is in Mexico City.
11. I have two (foot, feet).
12. My (tooth, teeth) is broken.
13. Those (child, children) have a cat.
14. The (man, men) has a house.
15. These (boy, boys) have a job.
16. The (men, mens) are at work.
17. The (children, childrens) are at school.
18. Those (women, womens) are beautiful.

Using Adjectives with *Have* and *Has*

As you know, an ***adjective*** is a word that modifies or describes something or someone. In this section, you'll learn how to use adjectives that describe your possessions. Consider this sentence:

> ▶ I have a **new** car. (Tengo un carro nuevo. Yo tengo un carro nuevo.)

Notice that, in the English sentence, you place the adjective, **new**, immediately <u>before</u> the noun it modifies. This is different from the Spanish translation in which you place the adjective <u>after</u> the noun.

In the following sentences, the adjectives in both English and Spanish are displayed in **bold** type.

> ▶ I have a **red** car. (Tengo un carro **rojo**.)

> ▶ My sister has a **pretty** daughter. (Mi hermana tiene una hija **bonita**.)

> ▶ She has two **pretty** dresses. (Ella tiene dos vestidos **bonitos**.)

Note that the spelling of the adjective **pretty** is the same whether it refers to one dress or two and that the adjective **two** comes before the adjective **pretty**.

Here are some examples of correct and incorrect English sentences that use adjectives. Do you know why the sentences in the right column are incorrect?

Correct sentences	Incorrect sentences
I have a red shirt. (Tengo una camisa roja.)	**I have a ~~shirt red~~.**
Joe has a clean house. (Joe tiene una casa limpia.)	**Joe has a ~~house clean~~.**
We have a new car. (Tenemos un carro nuevo.)	**We have a ~~car new~~.**

This list shows you more vocabulary used to describe appearance.

Vocabulary: Appearance	
black hair (pelo negro)	**curly hair** (pelo rizado)
brown hair (pelo castaño)	**blue eyes** (ojos de color azul)
short hair (pelo corto)	**brown eyes** (ojos de color café)
long hair (pelo largo)	**black eyes** (ojos de color negro)
straight hair (pelo lacio)	**green eyes** (ojos de color verde)

Hair (pelo) is a special kind of noun called a ***no-count noun*** that is singular but isn't preceded by **a**. Thus you say

> ▶ I have black hair. (Tengo pelo negro.)

You don't say

> ▶ ~~I have a black hair~~.

4.5.a Directions: Make a correct sentence by underlining either **have** or **has**.

1. Amanda (have, <u>has</u>) a good job.

2. The sisters (have, has) brown eyes.

3. The men (have, has) curly hair.

4. The students (have, has) an interesting class.

5. Ernesto (have, has) black hair.

6. Anna (have, has) long hair.

7. I (have, has) blue eyes.

8. The people (have, has) a big garden.

9. María (have, has) a handsome boyfriend.

10. The man (have, has) two sisters and one brother.

4.5.b Directions: One of the sentences in each line is not correct. Cross out the **incorrect** sentence.

1a. ~~I have a dress new.~~

2a. Ana has a beautiful house.

3a. The school has chairs blue.

4a. I have a good boss (jefe).

5a. I have eyes of color blue.

6a. Ana has hair straight.

7a. She has two new dresses.

8a. We have goods teachers.

1b. I have a new dress.

2b. Ana has a house beautiful.

3b. The school has blue chairs.

4b. I have a boss good.

5b. I have blue eyes.

6b. Ana has straight hair.

7b. She has two new dress.

8b. We have good teachers.

4.5.c Directions: Complete each sentence using **have** or **has** and **a** or **an**.

1. The boys __have__ __an__ interesting book.

2. The teacher _____ lazy student.

3. You _____ clean house.

4. The engineer _____ good job.

5. My friend _____ _____ old backpack.

6. We _____ expensive car.

7. I _____ beautiful garden.

8. They _____ nice friend.

4.5.d Directions: Translate these sentences.

1. Él tiene un carro blanco. __He has a white car.__

2. Susan tiene un libro nuevo. _____

3. Tenemos amigos de Chicago. _____

4. Mi hermana tiene ojos de color negro. _____

5. Él tiene un gato negro. _____

6. Tengo pelo corto. _____

7. Tú tienes una hermana inteligente. _____

4.6   *To Have vs. To Be*

You have now learned to use two of the most important verbs in the English language: **to have** and **to be**. In general, you use these verbs in much the same way that they are used in Spanish. The following table summarizes the uses of these verbs that you have learned thus far.

Use of to have		Uses of to be	
When to use	**Examples**	**When to use**	**Examples**
To show that something belongs to or is associated with someone or something	That man **has** a new car. We **have** two brothers.	To state one's place of origin	He **is** from New York.
		To describe a person, place, or thing	Anna **is** beautiful. He **is** hardworking.
		To state one's job	We **are** babysitters.

There are, however, some important instances when you use tener in Spanish but you use **to be** in English. Study these examples:

*Tengo calor.

*Tengo frío.

*Tengo hambre.

*Tengo sed.

Here are more examples:

Vocabulary: Expressions with to be	
I **am** lucky.	**Tengo** suerte.
I **am** sleepy.	**Tengo** sueño.
I **am** afraid.	**Tengo** miedo.

4.6.a Directions: Write the letter of the phrase in Column 2 that translates to the phrase in Column 1.

Column 1	Column 2
1. I am afraid. _D_	A. Tengo suerte.
2. I am cold. _____	B. Tengo frío.
3. I am hungry. _____	C. Tengo calor.
4. I am hot. _____	D. Tengo miedo.
5. I am lucky. _____	E. Tengo sed.
6. I am thirsty. _____	F. Tengo hambre.
7. I am sleepy. _____	G. Tengo sueño.

4.6.b Directions: Complete each sentence with the correct form of **to be** or **to have**.

1. Lydia __has__ three sisters.
2. The teachers __are__ hardworking.
3. I _____ a good job.
4. We _____ tired.
5. The woman _____ in love.
6. Those people _____ a beautiful house.
7. Those men _____ from Guatemala.
8. That backpack _____ blue and white.
9. Edgar and I _____ two cats.
10. The table _____ broken.
11. The cherries _____ good.
12. Luciano _____ a big family.
13. Miguel and I _____ married.
14. Frida _____ long, brown hair and brown eyes.
15. The women _____ beautiful.
16. Those people _____ cashiers.
17. That child _____ short hair.
18. I _____ two jobs (trabajos).
19. That car _____ dirty.
20. Gabriel _____ three apples and two peaches.

4.6.c Directions: Translate these sentences.

1. Conci está enferma. ___Conci is sick.___
2. Lillian tiene un vestido nuevo. _____
3. Ellos tienen dos trabajos (jobs). _____
4. La casa está limpia. _____
5. Mi novio es guapo. _____
6. Elvira tiene un carro viejo. _____
7. Enrique y yo tenemos dos hijas. _____
8. Los hombres son flojos. _____

Age is another example in which you use the verb tener in Spanish and the verb **to be** in English. Study this conversation.

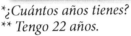

*¿Cuántos años tienes?
** Tengo 22 años.

*¿Cuántos años tienes?
** Tengo 22 años también.

*¿Cuántos años tiene tu hijo?
** Él tiene dos años.

Notice that you never say

▶ I have 22 years old.

▶ I am 22 years.

▶ My son has 4 years old.

▶ My son is 22 years.

To speak about your age, you need to learn more numbers, so here they are.

Vocabulary: Numbers from 11 to 100			
11 eleven	20 twenty	29 twenty-nine	70 seventy
12 twelve	21 twenty-one	30 thirty	71 seventy-one
13 thirteen	22 twenty-two	31 thirty-one	80 eighty
14 fourteen	23 twenty-three	40 forty	81 eighty-one
15 fifteen	24 twenty-four	41 forty-one	90 ninety
16 sixteen	25 twenty-five	50 fifty	91 ninety-one
17 seventeen	26 twenty-six	51 fifty-one	100 one hundred
18 eighteen	27 twenty-seven	60 sixty	
19 nineteen	28 twenty-eight	61 sixty-one	

The numbers that are two words are separated by a hyphen (-). These include the numbers from twenty-one to twenty-nine, thirty-one to thirty-nine, and so on.

4.7a Directions: Write the correct number after the numeral.

1. 22 _twenty-two_   6. 16 _____   11. 19 _____   16. 34 _____

2. 41 _____   7. 58 _____   12. 84 _____   17. 99 _____

3. 62 _____   8. 12 _____   13. 90 _____   18. 100 _____

4. 54 _____   9. 18 _____   14. 11 _____   19. 40 _____

5. 70 _____   10. 14 _____   15. 13 _____   20. 77 _____

4.7.b Directions: One of the sentences in each line is not correct. Cross out the **incorrect** sentence.

1a. ~~Lucas has 24 years.~~   1b. Lucas is 24 years old.

2a. I have 19 years old.   2b. I am 19 years old.

3a. We are 44.   3b. We have 44.

4a. The women are 37 years old.   4b. The women is 37 years old.

5a. I am 22 years old.   5b. I am 22 years.

6a. That man is 97 years.   6b. That man is 97 years old.

7a. Lynn and I are 34.   7b. Lynn and I have 34.

8a. I have 17.   8b. I am 17.

4.7.c Directions: Read the list of students and their ages. Then answer the questions about students' ages.

Name	Age
Bernardo Rossini	20
Lucas Verbena	16
Pamela Rosen	19
Lucinda Black	18
Barbara Putney	19
Angi Sanchez	17
Peter Kemp	18

1. How old is Bernardo Rossini? _He is 20 years old._

2. How old is Lucas Verbena? _____

3. How old are Pamela Rosen and Barbara Putney? _____

4. How old is Angi Sanchez? _____

5. How old are Lucinda Black and Peter Kemp? _____

The Verb to have

You conjugate the verb **to have** (tener) this way:

I **have**	he **has**
you **have**	she **has**
we **have**	it **has**
they **have**	

Using a and an before adjectives

Use **a** before an adjective or singular noun that begins with a consonant and **an** before an adjective or singular noun that begins with a vowel.

- ► I have a new car.
- ► I have an old car.

You never use **a** or **an** before adjectives that proceed plural nouns.

- ► ~~We have a good books.~~

Adjectives that describe what you have

In sentences that tell what you have, the adjective comes <u>before</u> the noun.

- ► I have a **red** car. (Tengo un carro nuevo.)
- ► Laura has a **new** backpack. (Laura tiene una mochila nueva.)

Adjectives in English do not change their endings, regardless of what the adjective modifies.

- ► I have a **new** book. (Tengo un libro nuevo.)
- ► I have two **new** books. (Tengo dos libros nuevos.)

To be vs. to have

The following table shows some instances in which you use tener in Spanish but you use **to be** in English.

Vocabulary: Expressions with to be	
I **am** hungry.	Tengo hambre.
I **am** thirsty.	Tengo sed.
I **am** hot.	Tengo calor.
I **am** cold.	Tengo frío.
I **am** lucky.	Tengo suerte.
I **am** afraid.	Tengo miedo.
I **am** sleepy.	Tengo sueño.

You use the verb **to be** to state age.

- ► I am 24 years old.

You don't say

- ► ~~I have 24 years old.~~

☞ More Practice!

P4.a Directions: Complete each sentence using **have** or **has**.

1. My sister ___has___ a desk.

2. I _____ a nice (agradable) boyfriend.

3. She _____ a blue and green dress.

4. You _____ an interesting textbook.

5. They _____ two children.

6. My brother _____ a good teacher.

7. The teacher _____ hardworking students.

8. My parents _____ three children.

9. Ana _____ a nice garden.

10. Jose and Linda _____ a new car.

11. I _____ a new backpack.

12. The doctor _____ six dogs.

13. We _____ a clean house.

14. The man _____ a beautiful girlfriend.

15. I _____ a good life (vida).

P4.b Directions: Write **S** if the noun is singular and **P** if the noun is plural.

1. child   S

2. women _____

3. tooth _____

4. foot _____

5. man _____

6. people _____

7. men _____

8. children _____

9. feet _____

10. teeth _____

11. person _____

12. woman _____

P4.c Directions: Write the correct number after the numeral.

1. 22   twenty-two

2. 43 _____

3. 65 _____

4. 86 _____

5. 11 _____

6. 91 _____

7. 85 _____

8. 30 _____

9. 49 _____

10. 14 _____

11. 18 _____

12. 86 _____

13. 64 _____

14. 77 _____

15. 36 _____

16. 34 _____

17. 55 _____

18. 100 _____

19. 90 _____

20. 47 _____

P4.d Directions: Make each singular noun plural.

1. party __parties__
2. city _____
3. dress _____
4. man _____
5. class _____
6. girl _____
7. church _____
8. child _____
9. aunt _____
10. boy _____

11. kiss _____
12. peach _____
13. lady _____
14. baby _____
15. foot _____
16. eraser _____
17. tooth _____
18. notebook _____
19. woman _____
20. cherry _____

P4.e Directions: One of the sentences in each pair is not a correct sentence. Cross out the **incorrect** sentence.

1a. ~~I have a two sisters.~~
2a. María has a nice house.
3a. I have a apple.
4a. We have a good teacher.
5a. Juan has four textbook.
6a. Laura has beautiful dresses.
7a. I have a problem big.
8a. Lisa has three dogs.
9a. I am healthy.
10a. They have friend in Utah.
11a. The childs are tired.
12a. The men are sick.
13a. He's a good boy.
14a. She has 16 years.
15a. The women are from NY.

1b. I have two sisters.
2b. María has nice house.
3b. I have an apple.
4b. We have a teacher good.
5b. Juan has four textbooks.
6b. Laura has dresses beautiful.
7b. I have a big problem.
8b. Lisa has three dog.
9b. I have healthy.
10b. They have a friend in Utah.
11b. The children are tired.
12b. The men have sick.
13b. He's a boy good.
14b. She is 16 years old.
15b. The womens are from NY.

P4.f Directions: Complete each sentence with the correct form of **to be** or **to have**.

1. Alfonso __has__ a big house.
2. The students ___are___ hardworking.
3. She _____ a good job.
4. They _____ in love.
5. The woman _____ two children.

6. I _____ a beautiful garden.
7. That man _____ from Peru.
8. The erasers _____ white.
9. Louisa _____ a brown dog.
10. I _____ a beautiful garden.

English Grammar: Step by Step 1

11. That peach _____ big.

12. Cecilia _____ brown eyes.

13. I _____ 24 years old.

14. Francisco and I _____ two children.

15. The child _____ a new book.

16. Martha _____ 45 years old.

P4.g Directions: Each sentence contains one error, which is underlined. Rewrite the sentence with the error corrected.

1. Susan <u>has</u> 30 years old.   Susan is 30 years old.

2. Marco <u>has</u> 24 years old. _____

3. Angel and Lupita <u>are</u> three children. _____

4. I am <u>no</u> in love. _____

5. We have a <u>daughter sick</u>. _____

6. Anna <u>has</u> 14 years old. _____

7. Linda and I <u>have</u> happy. _____

8. The men <u>no are</u> from Cuba. _____

P4.h Directions: Read the paragraph. Then answer the questions using complete sentences. <u>Use contractions where you can.</u>

Lucas is from El Salvador. He is 55 years old. He has long, curly hair and black eyes. He is short and heavy. He is a gardener (*jardinero*). He is hardworking. He is married and he has two children, a son and a daughter. His daughter is married. She has two children, Michael and Anna. Michael is 10 years old and Anna is 8 years old. Lucas also (*también*) has a lazy dog. Her name is Lulu. She is 12 years old.

1. How old is Lucas?   He's 55 years old. _____

2. Is Lucas a construction worker? _____

3. What is his job? _____

4. How old is Michael? _____

5. How old is Anna? _____

6. How old is the dog? _____

7. Is Lucas a grandfather (abuelo)? _____

8. Is Lucas young? _____

9. Is Lucas single? _____

10. Where is Lucas from? _____

Chapter 5

My last name is Vargas.

While you may not realize it, some of the most commonly used words in a language pertain to how people are related and what belongs to whom. Imagine, for example, if you had no way to introduce a spouse to a friend or no way of explaining that a particular possession belonged to you. This chapter focuses on possessive adjectives, the words that let us communicate these important relationships.

At the end of the chapter you will know how to

- talk about members of your family, such as aunts, uncles, and cousins.
- use possessive adjectives to describe what belongs to whom.
- answer questions about your first, middle, and last name.

You use *possessive adjectives* to show that something belongs to someone. In the phrase **my book, my** is an adjective because it modifies the noun **book**. It is a *possessive adjective* because it tells who owns, or possesses, the book. In both English and Spanish, each possessive adjective is associated with a subject pronoun. Study this table.

Subject pronouns	Possessive adjectives in English	Possessive adjectives in Spanish
I (yo)	**my**	mi, mis
you (tú, usted)	**your**	tu, tus, su, sus
he (él)	**his**	su (de él), sus (de él)
she (ella)	**her**	su (de ella), sus (de ella)
it	**its**	su
we (nosotros, nosotras)	**our**	nuestro, nuestra, nuestros, nuestras
they (ellos, ellas)	**their**	su (de ellos), su (de ellas), sus (de ellos), sus (de ellas)

Let's begin with the possessive adjective **my**. As the table above indicates, **my** means both *mi* and *mis*. Study these sentences:

*Mi gato es negro.   *Mis perros son blancos.

Notice that, in both English sentences, **my** is the possessive adjective; it doesn't matter whether what is possessed is singular or plural.

You often use the names of family members with possessive adjectives, so study these words.

Vocabulary: Members of the family		
wife (esposa)	**aunt** (tía)	**grandmother** (abuela)
husband (esposo)	**uncle** (tío)	**grandfather** (abuelo)
daughter (hija)	**niece** (sobrina)	**granddaughter** (nieta)
son (hijo)	**nephew** (sobrino)	**grandson** (nieto)
parents (padres)	**cousin*** (prima, primo)	**relatives** (parientes, familiares)

*The English word for primo, **cousin**, refers to a male or a female. Similarly, **cousins** refers to more than one **cousin**, regardless of gender.

5.1.a Directions: This table lists female family members. Write the names of the associated male family member in the space provided.

1. sister   brother   5. daughter _____

2. mother _____   6. grandmother _____

3. aunt _____   7. granddaughter _____

4. wife _____   8. niece _____

5.1.b Directions: This table lists male family members. Write the name of the associated female family member in the space provided.

1. father   mother   5. nephew _____

2. husband _____   6. grandson _____

3. brother _____   7. uncle _____

4. grandfather _____   8. son _____

5.1.c Directions: Translate the names of these family members.

1. mi hermana   my sister   6. mis tías _____

2. mis hermanas   my sisters   7. mis padres _____

3. mi hermano _____   8. mi tío _____

4. mis hermanos _____   9. mi prima _____

5. mi tía _____   10. mi primo _____

5.1.d Directions: Translate these sentences.

1. Mi tía es de San Francisco.   My aunt is from San Francisco.

2. Mi prima tiene ojos de color negro. _____

3. Mis hermanas son de Guadalajara. _____

4. Mis niños son inteligentes. _____

5. Mi abuela es vieja. _____

6. Mi esposo tiene pelo de color negro. _____

7. Mis amigas tienen un carro nuevo. _____

8. Mis nietas son trabajadoras. _____

9. Mi tía es de Lima. _____

10. Mi sobrino es cajero. _____

In this section you'll learn to use the possessive adjectives **his** and **her**.

► **his** means su (de él) and sus (de él)

► **her** means su (de ella) and sus (de ella)

Look at the following drawings:

Marco has a cat.
(Marco tiene un gato.)
His cat is black.
(Su gato es negro.)

Marco has two dogs.
(Marco tiene dos perros.)
His dogs are black.
(Sus perros son negros.)

In both sentences, you use the possessive adjective **his** because the animals belong to Marco, who is male. Now study these drawings:

Amanda has a cat.
(Amanda tiene un gato.)
Her cat is white.
(Su gato es blanco.)

Amanda has two dogs.
(Amanda tiene dos perros.)
Her dogs are white.
(Sus perros son blancos.)

In these sentences, you use the possessive adjective **her** because both the dog and cat belong to Amanda, who is female.

Rule of grammar: In English, the possessive adjective you use is determined by the possessor, that is, who possesses the noun that follows.

Common mistakes with his and he
People who are learning English often use the pronoun **he** when they should use **his**. For example, it is common for people to say

► ~~He brother is a teacher.~~

What they should say is

► His brother is a teacher. (Su hermano es maestro. El hermano de él es maestro.)

5.2.a Directions: Complete the sentences with **my, his** or **her**.

1. She has a book. ___Her___ book is interesting.

2. She has a job. _____ job is good.

3. I have a house _____ house is small.

4. Martin has a dog. _____ dog is brown and white.

5. He has beautiful eyes. _____ eyes are big and black.

6. I have a sister. _____ sister is beautiful.

7. Ana has a boyfriend. _____ boyfriend has brown hair and blue eyes.

8. Raymundo has a girlfriend. _____ girlfriend is a nurse.

9. Leo has a new textbook. _____ textbook is interesting.

10. Anita has beautiful hair. _____ hair is long and curly.

11. Alice has a job. _____ job is interesting.

12. I have two cousins. _____ cousins are cooks.

5.2.b Directions: Complete the sentences in the paragraph with **my, his** or **her**.

___My___ name is Emily. I have a sister. _____ name is Lisa. I have a brother. _____ name is Arturo.
⟨1.⟩   ⟨2.⟩   ⟨3.⟩

Arturo is married. _____ wife is Rebecca.
                    ⟨4.⟩

5.2.c Directions: Replace each blank with **he** or **his**.

1. ___He___ is my friend.   3. _____ has a good job.   5. _____ shirt (camisa) is red.

2. _____ friend is from Japan.   4. _____ is in love.   6. _____ name is Juan.

5.2.d Directions: Replace each blank with **she** or **her**.

1. ___She___ is a homemaker.   3. _____ sister is a nurse.   5. _____ dress is beautiful.

2. _____ has two sisters.   4. _____ has a big problem.   6. _____ name is Sandra.

5.2.e Directions: Translate these sentences.

1. La casa de él está limpia. ___His house is clean.___

2. La casa de ella está limpia. _____

3. El carro de él está sucio. _____

4. El carro de ella está sucio. _____

5. La maestra de ella es muy (very) bonita. _____

More Possesive Adjectives: *Your* and *Our*

In this section, you'll learn about two more possessive adjectives: **your** and **our**.

The possessive adjective **your**

You use the possessive adjective **your** (tu, tus, su, and sus) when a possession belongs to the person you are talking to. Study these examples:

*Tus zapatos son bonitos.   **Tu carro es bonito.*

Note that you use the same pronoun, **your**, whether the noun that follows is singular or plural.

Your vs. You're

While **your** and **you're** have the same pronunciation, their meanings are different. **Your** is a possessive adjective used to indicate that something belongs to the person you're talking to. For example, you might say

▶ **Your** friend is from Mexico. (Tu amigo es de México.)

In contrast, **you're** is a contraction that means **you are**. You might say

▶ **You're** my friend. (Tú eres mi amigo.)

The possessive adjective **our**

The possessive adjective **our** is used for nuestro, nuestra, nuestros, and nuestras. Here are some examples:

▶ Luis and I have a car. **Our** car is broken. (Luis y yo tenemos un carro. **Nuestro** carro está roto.)

▶ Luis and I have two cars. **Our** cars are broken. (Luis y yo tenemos dos carros. **Nuestros** carros están rotos.)

Here again, you use the same possessive adjective, **our**, regardless of the noun that follows.

5.3.a Directions: Complete the sentences with the possessive adjective **my, his, her, your** or **our.**

1. Martin and I have a textbook. ___Our___ textbook is interesting.

2. Raymondo and I have two daughters. _____ daughters are in Guatemala.

3. You are lucky. You have two bicycles. _____ bicycles are new.

4. Juan has a car. _____ car is new.

5. I have a boyfriend (novio). _____ boyfriend is handsome.

6. My nephew has a girlfriend (novia). _____ girlfriend is beautiful.

7. You have a garden. _____ garden is big.

8. My niece has a dog. _____ dog is black.

5.3.b Directions: Complete the sentences with **you, your, we** or **our.**

1. We are from the United States. ___Our___ grandmother is from France.

2. Janet and I are teachers. _____ are happy.

3. You are beautiful. _____ also (también) are a good person.

4. Bernice and I are friends. _____ husbands are friends also.

5. My uncle and I are hungry. _____ also are tired.

6. You are a salesperson. _____ have a difficult job.

7. Adam and I are in love. _____ are happy.

8. You have a good husband. _____ husband has a good wife.

5.3.c Directions: Make a correct sentence by underlining either **your** or **you're.**

1. (Your, <u>You're</u>) from Chicago.   4. (Your, You're) a homemaker.

2. (Your, You're) a good person.   5. Is (your, you're) aunt a doctor?

3. (Your, You're) beautiful.   6. (Your, You're) dog is black.

5.3.d Directions: Translate these sentences.

1. Tu sobrino es guapo. ___Your nephew is handsome.___

2. Tu jardín es bonito. _____

3. Las niñas de ella son inteligentes. _____

4. Tus primos son de Dallas. _____

5. Juan y yo estamos cansados. Nuestros trabajos son difíciles. _____

6. Cecilia y yo somos amigas. Nuestras madres son amigas también (also). _____

More Possessive Adjectives: *Its* and *Their*

In this section, you'll learn about the final possessive adjectives: **its** and **their**.

The possessive adjective its

The possessive adjective **its** is used to show that something belongs to another object or to an animal. Here is an example:

*Tengo un pez. Su nombre es Bobo.

The possessive adjective their

You use the possessive adjective **their** to refer to people and things that are possessed by more than one person other than you. **Their** has these meanings in Spansh:

- ▶ su (de ellas o de ellos)
- ▶ sus (de ellas o de ellos)

Here are some examples of how **their** is used:

- ▶ My parents have a dog. **Their** dog is big. (Mis padres tienen un perro. Su perro es grande.)
- ▶ My parents have two dogs. **Their** dogs are big. (Mis padres tienen dos perros. Sus perros son grandes.)

Their vs. They're

Their and **they're** are pronounced the same way but have different meanings. **Their** is a possessive adjective. For example,

- ▶ **Their** mother has two children. (Su madre tiene dos niños. La madre de ellos tiene dos niños.)

They're is a contraction that means **they are**. For example,

- ▶ **They're** from New York. (Ellos son de Nueva York.)

Language subtleties: A third word, **there**, is pronounced the same way as **their** and **they're**. **There** means allí. It also is similar to hay.

5.4.a Directions: Complete the sentences with the possessive adjective **his, her** or **their**.

1. Martin and Edward have a textbook. ___Their___ textbook is interesting.

2. Linda and Manuel have two daughters. _____ daughters are in Oregon.

3. Arnold has two bicycles. _____ bicycles are new.

4. My niece is a teacher. _____ job is difficult.

5. Peter and Alejandro have a dog. _____ dog is very (muy) sick.

6. Isabel has a boyfriend. _____ boyfriend is hardworking.

7. The brothers have a new job. _____ job is easy (fácil).

8. My niece has a dog. _____ dog is always (siempre) hungry.

9. Edgar has eleven uncles. _____ family is very big.

10. My aunt is from Argentina but (pero) _____ English is good.

5.4.b Directions: : Complete the sentences with **he, his, she, her, they** or **their**.

1. My brothers have a car but ___their___ car is always broken.

2. Flora and Ray aren't cooks. _____ are waiters.

3. Arnoldo and Lola have two children. _____ also have two dogs.

4. My aunt has a new blouse (blusa). _____ blouse is beautiful.

5. Martin is a doctor. _____ job is difficult (difícil).

6. Laura and Miguel have a new house. _____ house is always cold.

7. Benito and Lulu have a fish. _____ fish is sick.

8. My grandfather is very old. _____ is hardworking too.

5.4.c Directions: Make a correct sentence by underlining either **their** or **they're**.

1. (Their, <u>They're</u>) from NY.

2. (Their, They're) here (aquí).

3. (Their, They're) my friends.

4. (Their, They're) names are Al and Max.

5. (Their, They're) sister is sick.

6. (Their, They're) car is broken.

5.4.d Directions: Translate these sentences.

1. Anna y Mario tienen una casa. Su casa es bonita. __Anna and Maria have a house. Their house is pretty.__

2. Mis primos tienen un jardín. Su jardín es bonito. _____

3. Mi tía y mi tío tienen un carro. Su carro está roto. _____

4. Mis padres tienen una casa grande. Su casa está en Michoacán. _____

5.5   Identifying your First, Middle, and Last Name

Now that you have some knowledge of English grammar, you're ready to identify yourself! This table lists the kinds of name-related questions you may be asked. The person answering the questions is a woman named **Ana Vargas González**.

What is your name?* (¿Cómo te llamas? ¿Cuál es tu nombre?)	**My name is Ana Vargas Gonzalez.** (Mi nombre es Ana Vargas González.)
What is your first name? (¿Cuál es tu primer nombre?)	**My first name is Ana.** (Mi primer nombre es Ana.)
What is your last name? (¿Cuál es tu apellido?)	**My last name is Gonzalez.** (Mi apellido es González.)
What is your middle name? (¿Cuál es tu segundo nombre?)	**My middle name is Vargas.** (Mi segundo nombre es Vargas.)
What is your middle initial? (¿Cuál es la inicial de tu segundo nombre?)	**My middle initial is V.** (La inicial de mi segundo nombre es V.)
What is your full name? What is your complete name?** (¿Cuál es tu nombre completo?)	**My complete name is Ana Vargas Gonzalez.** (Mi nombre completo es Ana Vargas González.)

*If someone asks you your name in English, and it's a fairly formal situation, such as a job interview, you should reply with your complete name. If someone asks you your name in an informal situation, such as a party, you can reply with your first name only.

****Full name** and **complete name** both mean **nombre completo**.

Suppose you take your baby Hector to the pediatrician and the nurse asks

▶ **What is his name?** (¿Cuál es su nombre?)

You might then reply

▶ **His name is Hector Garcia Lopez.** (Su nombre es Héctor García López.)

If you had a baby daughter, the nurse might ask you

▶ **What is her name?** (¿Cuál es su nombre?)

You might then reply

▶ **Her name is Dulce Garcia Lopez.** (Su nombre es Dulce García López.)

If you had twins, the nurse might ask you

▶ **What are their names?** (¿Cuáles son sus nombres?)

You then would reply

▶ **Their names are Hector Luis Lopez and Dulce Garcia Lopez.** (Sus nombres son Héctor García López y Dulce García López.)

5.5.a Directions: Answer each question with a complete sentence.

 Juan Garcia Castro

 Patricia Ortiz Sanchez

1. What is his full name?   His full name is Juan Garcia Castro.

2. What is his first name?

3. What is his middle name?

4. What is his last name?

5. What is his middle initial?

6. What is her full name?

7. What is her first name?

8. What is her middle name?

9. What is her last name?

10. What is her middle initial?

11. What is your full name?

12. What is your first name?

13. What is your middle name?

14. What is your last name?

15. What is your middle initial?

5.5.b Directions: Use the following words to fill in the blanks. Cross out each word after you use it. Then practice the conversation with a friend.

~~your~~   am   name   a   I'm   years   job   you

Luis: What is __your__ name?
      1.
Anna: My _____ is Anna Garcia.
         2.
Luis: How old are you?

Anna: _____ 32 _____ old.
      3.   4.
Luis: What is your _____?
                    5.
Anna: I am _____ nurse.
          6.
Luis: Are _____ happy in the United States?
          7.
Anna: Yes, I _____
              8.

English Grammar: Step by Step 1   97

Chapter 5 Summary

Possessive adjectives

Possessive adjectives (adjetivos posesivos) are adjectives that show that something belongs to someone.

Subject pronouns	Possessive adjectives in English	Possessive adjectives in Spanish
I (yo)	**my**	mi, mis
you (tú, usted)	**your**	tu, tus, su, sus
he (él)	**his**	su (de él), sus (de él)
she (ella)	**her**	su (de ella), sus (de ella)
it	**its**	su
we (nosotros, nosotras)	**our**	nuestro, nuestra, nuestros, nuestras
they (ellos, ellas)	**their**	su (de ellos), su (de ellas), sus (de ellos), sus (de ellas)

In English the possessive adjective you use is determined by the possessor.

► Susan has a new car. **Her** car is expensive. (Susan tiene un carro nuevo. Su carro es costoso.)

► Mario has a new car. **His** car is expensive. (Mario tiene un carro nuevo. Su carro es costoso.)

First, middle and last names	
What is your name? (¿Cómo te llamas? ¿Cuál es tu nombre?)	**My name is Ana Vargas Gonzalez.** (Mi nombre es Ana Vargas González.)
What is your first name? (¿Cuál es tu primer nombre?)	**My first name is Ana.** (Mi primer nombre es Ana.)
What is your last name? (¿Cuál es tu apellido?)	**My last name is Gonzalez.** (Mi apellido es González.)
What is your middle name? (¿Cuál es tu segundo nombre?)	**My middle name is Vargas.** (Mi segundo nombre es Vargas.)
What is your middle initial? (¿Cuál es la inicial de tu segundo nombre?)	**My middle initial is V.** (La inicial de mi segundo nombre es V.)
What is your full name? **What is your complete name?** (¿Cuál es tu nombre completo?)	**My full name is Ana Vargas Gonzales.** (Mi nombre completo es Ana Vargas González.)

 *More Practice!*

P5.a Directions: Write whether each family member is male or female. Then, write the name of the family member of the "opposite" gender.

Relationship of family member	Is this family member masculine or feminine?	Name of person of the opposite gender
aunt	1a. feminine	1b. uncle
son	2a.	2b.
brother	3a.	3b.
grandmother	4a.	4b.
nephew	5a.	5b.

P5.b Directions: Complete the sentence with **my, your, his, her, its, our** or **their**.

_____My_____ name is Marcela. I am a student. _____ sister is a nurse. _____ name is
   1.   2.   3.
Barbara. _____ brother is a construction worker. _____ name is Marcos. Marcos is married.
                    4.   5.
_____ wife is Andrea. Marcos and Andrea have two children. _____ names are Isabel and
   6.   7.
Miguel. Isabel has a fish (un pez). _____ name is Happy. We live in a small house. _____
                              8.   9.
house is beautiful.

P5.c Directions: Complete the sentences with the possessive adjective **my, your, his, her, its our** or **their**.

1. Martin and I are teachers. ____Our____ job is interesting.

2. Linda and Manuel are nurses. _____ job is difficult.

3. I have two bicycles. _____ bicycles are new.

4. Angi is from Guatemala. _____ English is good.

5. Peter and I have a fish. _____ fish is orange.

6. Jesus has a girlfriend. _____ girlfriend is funny (chistosa).

7. My sisters have a new job. _____ job is in San Francisco.

8. My niece has a dog. _____ dog is always (siempre) thirsty.

P5.d Directions: Complete the sentences with **I, my, you, your, he, his, she** or **her**.

1. Laura is a teacher. ____Her____ job is interesting.

2. Janet is a teacher. _____ has a good job.

3. Mr. Lopez is from Nicaragua. _____ family is in the United States.

4. Mrs. Lopez is a nurse. _____ has three children.

5. I'm not tired, but _____ am hungry.

6. You are my friend. _____ husband is my friend also.

P5.e Directions: Only one of the responses is correct. Cross out the **incorrect** response.

1. Maria has a car.	1a. Her car is red.	1b. ~~His car is red.~~
2. Marco has a jacket.	2a. Her jacket is red.	2b. His jacket is red.
3. Maria and Miguel have a daughter.	3a. Their daughter is tired.	3b. Her daughter is tired.
4. I have an uncle.	4a. His uncle is healthy.	4b. My uncle is healthy.
5. My sisters have a car.	5a. Their car is new.	5b. My car is new.
6. Ana has a dress.	6a. Her dress is green.	6b. His dress is green.
7. Ana and Lisa have a brother.	7a. Their brother is handsome.	7b. Her brother is handsome.
8. We have a dog.	8a. Their dog is brown.	8b. Our dog is brown.
9. You have a nice family.	9a. Your family is big.	9b. Their family is big.
10. The man is worried. (preocupado)	10a. His daughter is sick.	10b. Her daughter is sick.

P5.f Directions: Translate these sentences into English.

1. Tenemos un carro blanco.

　　　We have a white car.

2. Nuestra sobrina es de Madrid.

3. Mi abuela tiene una casa grande.

4. Mi hermana tiene ojos de color azul.

5. El apellido de él es Márquez.

6. Nuestro trabajo es difícil.

7. El doctor es de Chicago. Su nombre es Paul.

8. La maestra es de New York. Su nombre es Louisa.

P5.g Directions: Complete the identification card for each of the people below. The first identification card is completed for you.

Identification Card 1: My name Angelica Martinez Torres. My address (*dirección*) is 45 Green Street. My city (*ciudad*) is Chicago. My state (*estado*) is Illinois. My zip code (*código postal*) is 68754. My telephone number (*número de teléfono*) is (312) 999-3357. My age (*edad*) is 44.

Identification Card 2: My name Luis Jonathan Alvarez. My address is 15 First Avenue. My city is Placerville. My state is Georgia and my zip code is 32333. My telephone number is (646) 644-1245. I am 24 years old.

Identification Card 3: My name Cynthia Martinez Fox. My address is 576 University Ave. My city is White Plains. My state is New York and my zip code is 10605. My telephone number is (924) 655-1246. My age is 31.

Identification Card 4: Complete the card for yourself.

IDENTIFICATION CARD 1

FIRST NAME   Angelica

MIDDLE INITIAL   M.

LAST NAME   Torres

STREET ADDRESS   45 Green Street

CITY   Chicago

STATE   Illinois   ZIP   68795

TELEPHONE NUMBER   (312) 999-3357

AGE   44

IDENTIFICATION CARD 2

FIRST NAME

MIDDLE INITIAL

LAST NAME

STREET ADDRESS

CITY

STATE   ZIP

TELEPHONE NUMBER

AGE

IDENTIFICATION CARD 3

FIRST NAME

MIDDLE INITIAL

LAST NAME

STREET ADDRESS

CITY

STATE   ZIP

TELEPHONE NUMBER

AGE

IDENTIFICATION CARD 4

FIRST NAME

MIDDLE INITIAL

LAST NAME

STREET ADDRESS

CITY

STATE   ZIP

TELEPHONE NUMBER

AGE

Appendix A: Answers to the Exercises

Chapter 1

1.1.a 1a. Laura 1b. perro 1c. gatos 2a. arroz
2b. frijoles 3a. paloma 3b. jardín 4a.
estudiantes 4b. aula 5a. casa 6a. Miguel
6b. Ernesto 6c. amigos 7a. lápiz 7b. mesa
8a. Juan 8b. Chicago

1.1.b 1. the chair 2. the store 3. the book
4. the girl 5. the table 6. the teacher
7. the house 8. the student 9. the school
10. the car 11. the boy 12. the teacher

1.2.a 1. S 2. P 3. S 4. P 5. P 6. S 7. S 8. P 9. P
10. S 11. S 12. P 13. P 14. S 15. S 16. P
17. S 18. P 19. S 20. P 21. P 22. S

1.2.b 1. the nurses 2. the teachers 3. the students
4. the stores 5. the dogs 6. the chairs
7. the books 8. the houses 9. the cars
10. the tables 11. the schools 12. the brothers

1.2.c 1. the table 2. the tables 3. the dog
4. the brothers 5. the cat 6. the chairs
7. the teacher 8. the books 9. the chair
10. the teachers 11. the mother
12. the houses 13. the cars 14. the student
15. the student 16. the students
17. the students 18. the sisters

1.3.a 1. S 2. P 3. P 4. S 5. P 6. S 7. S 8. P 9. S
10. P 11. S 12. P 13. P 14. P 15. S 16. S

1.3.b 1. El estudiante es 2. Ellos están
3. Nosotras somos 4. La maestra está
5. Las sillas son 6. El vecindario es
7. El carro está 8. Los estudiantes están
9. Yo soy 10. Alex y yo somos
11. Jennifer Lopez es 12. Las montañas son
13. Las mujeres están 14. Enrique y yo somos
15. Los perros están 16. Los libros están
17. La tienda está 18. Lucas está

1.4.a 1. ellos ellas 2. él 3. yo 4. nosotros nosotras
5. tú usted ustedes 6. ella

1.4.b 1. he 2. she 3. I 4. they 5. we 6. you

1.4.c 1. she 2. you 3. he 4. she 5. they 6. you
7. I 8. you 9. we 10. they

1.4.d 1. she 2. he 3. they 4. they 5. she
6. they 7. they 8. he 9. she 10. they 11. he
12. they 13. they 14. she 15. they 16. he

1.5.a 1. He is from San Luis Potosi. 2. Linda is from
Zacatecas. 3. Anna is from Nicaragua.
4. Peter is from Ecuador. 5. Jesus is from
Cuba. 6. Wendy is from Chihuahua.
7. Dulce is from Guerrero. 8. Francisco is
from Campeche. 9. Gabriela is from Hidalgo.
10. Edgar is from Coahuila.

1.5.b. 1b. ~~I from Bolivia.~~ 2a. ~~I from New York.~~
3a. ~~My from is Spain.~~ 4a. ~~I from Guatemala.~~
5b. ~~Am from Seattle.~~ 6a. ~~I from Equador.~~
7a. ~~Am de Mexico.~~

1.5.c 1. I am from San Salvador. 2. I am from San
Salvador. 3. I am from Honduras. 4. I am
from Chiapas. 5. I am from Chiapas.

1.6.a 1. am 2. is 3. is 4. is 5. is 6. is 7. is
8. am 9. is 10. am

1.6.b 1. He 2. She 3. She 4. She 5. He

1.6.c 1b. ~~She am from England.~~ 2a. ~~I is from New York.~~ 3a. ~~Is from Miami.~~ 4b. ~~Is from Chicago.~~
5b. ~~Am from Madrid.~~

1.6.d 1. Susan is from San Salvador. 2. Juan is from
Michoacan. 3. My brother is from León.
4. He is from Guadalajara. 5. I am from
Oaxaca. 6. The boy is from Hawaii.

1.7.a 1. am 2. are 3. is 4. is 5. are 6. are 7. are
8. is 9. am 10. is 11. are 12. are 13. is 14. are
15. are 16. am 17. are 18. is 19. are 20. are

1.7.b 1. Susan is from San Salvador. 2. Juan and
Nancy are from Chicago. 3. My sister is from
Dallas. 4. They are from Lima. 5. We are from

San Juan.

1.7.c 1b. ~~She are from England.~~ 2a. ~~I are from New York.~~ 3a. ~~We is from Miami.~~ 4b. ~~He are from Chicago.~~ 5b. ~~The boys am from Cuba.~~ 6a. ~~My from is Madrid.~~ 7a. ~~You is from Toyko.~~ 8a. ~~Lourdes are from Taiwan.~~

1.8.a 1a. ~~Susan she is from NY.~~ 2b. ~~Bob he is from Boston.~~ 3c. ~~Lily she is from Reno.~~ 4b. ~~Dan he is from Peru.~~ 5a. ~~The girls they are from LA.~~

1.8.b 1a. ~~Is from NY.~~ 2a. ~~Jose he is from Ecatepec.~~ 3a. ~~Are from Ciudad Juárez.~~ 4a. ~~Is from Saltillo.~~ 5a. ~~Lisa she is from Monterrey.~~ 6b. ~~Are from San Luis Potosí.~~ 7a. ~~I am NY.~~ 8a. ~~Ernesto is Guadalajara.~~ 9a. ~~Louisa and Anita from LA.~~ 10b. ~~He is Guatemala City.~~ 11a. ~~Lisa from Culiacan.~~ 12b. ~~We from Zapopan.~~ 13a. ~~I from Nezahualcoytl.~~ 14a. ~~They are Guadalupe.~~

1.8.c 1. am 2. are 3. is 4. are 5. are 6. are 7. are 8. is

P1.a 1. sons 2. daughters 3. friends 4. boys 5. books 6. sisters 7. teachers 8. girls

P1.b 1. P 2. S 3. S 4. P 5. S 6. S 7. S 8. P 9. P 10. S 11. S 12. P 13. S 14. P 15. S 16. P

P1.c 1. <u>Mi hermana</u> <u>está</u> 2. <u>Ellos</u> <u>son</u> 3. <u>El libro</u> <u>es</u> 4. <u>Ella</u> <u>está</u> 5. <u>Enrique</u> <u>es</u> 6. <u>Nosotros</u> <u>estamos</u> 7. <u>La fiesta</u> <u>es</u> 8. <u>Las mujeres</u> <u>son</u> 9. <u>El</u> <u>es</u> 10. <u>Las maestras</u> <u>están</u>

P1.d 1. they 2. I 3. we 4. you 5. she 6. he 7. you 8. they 9. we 10. you

P1.e 1. is 2. are 3. is 4. are 5. are 6. are 7. are 8. is 9. is 10. is 11. am 12. is 13. are 14. is 15. am 16. is 17. is 18. are 19. is 20. am

P1.f 1. The girls are from Mexico. 2. The boys are from India. 3. The teachers are from Guatemala. 4. The girls are from Bolivia 5. The doctors are from El Salvador. 6. The students are from San Francisco.

P1.g 1a. ~~I am Chicago.~~ 2b. ~~Ernesto he is from Guadalahara.~~ 3a. ~~Louisa and Anita from LA.~~ 4a. ~~Is from Guatemala City.~~ 5b. ~~Lisa she is from Haiti.~~ 6b. ~~We from Caracas.~~

7a. ~~I from Mexico City.~~ 8a. ~~Louisa she is from~~

~~Guadalupe.~~ 9a. ~~He from United States.~~ 10b. ~~My brother he from Boston.~~

P1.h 1. They are from New York. 2. She is from Panama. 3. They are from Brazil. 4. He is from Argentina. 5. They are from Alaska. 6. They are from Las Vegas. 7. He is from the United States. 8. She is from Mexico City.

P1.i 1. She is from Nicaragua. 2. We are from San Diego. 3. The girls are from Chicago. 4. The teacher is from Guadalajara. 5. They are from Cancun. 6. The students are from Bogota. 7. I am from San Francisco. 8. The teachers are from Houston.

Chapter 2

2.1.a 1. V 2. C 3. C 4. C 5. C 6. V 7. C 8. C 9. V 10. C 11. C 12. C 13. V 14. C 15. C 16. V 17. C 18. C 19. C 20. C

2.1.b 1. a 2. an 3. an 4. a 5. a 6. a 7. an 8. a 9. an 10. a 11. a 12. a 13. an 14. a 15. a 16. a 17. an 18. a 19. an 20. a

2.1.c 1a. ~~a egg~~ 2b. ~~an book~~ 3a. ~~a opera~~ 4b. ~~an chair~~ 5b. ~~an student~~ 6a. ~~a apple~~

2.1.d 1. the cat 2. a cat 3. the house 4. a house 5. a teacher 6. the teacher 7. the teachers 8. the cats 9. the stores 10. the store 11. a store 12. the chair 13. a girl 14. the girl 15. the girls 16. a chair

2.2.a 1. a 2. a 3. an 4. a 5. a 6. an 7. a 8. a 9. a 10. a 11. a 12. a 13. an 14. a 15. a 16. a

2.2.b 1. I am a doctor. 2. Anna is a cashier. 3. Juan is a teacher. 4. My brother is a waiter. 5. Juan is a construction worker. 6. He is an engineer. 7. Maria is from Cuba. 8. Lucas is a salesperson. 9. Lily is a salesperson. 10. Sandra is a homemaker. 11. I am a babysitter. 12. My mother is an engineer.

2.2.c 1b. ~~I am an doctor.~~ 2a. ~~Anna is a artist.~~ 3b. ~~Caroline is an doctor.~~ 4a. ~~Marco is a engineer.~~ 5b. ~~Tom is from a San Pablo.~~ 6b. ~~Laura is an nurse.~~

2.3.a 1b. ~~They are a waiters.~~ 2a. ~~Anna and Amy are artist.~~ 3b. ~~Coco and Adam are teacher.~~ 4a. ~~They are a engineers.~~ 5b. ~~Tom is nurse.~~ 6b. ~~Miguel and Anna are cook.~~ 7a. ~~He is a engineer.~~ 8b. ~~They are a artists.~~

2.3.b 1. They are doctors. 2. They are students. 3. They are nurses. 4. They are nurses. 5. The girls are students. 6. The boys are students. 7. The girls are artists. 8. The boys are artists.

2.3.c 1. They are engineers. 2. They are cashiers. 3. Marvin and Amanda are artists. 4. My sister is a waitress. 5. Juana and Adam are cooks. 6. I am a cook. 7. Louisa is an artist. 8. Luis is a salesperson. 9. Lily and Chelsea are nurses. 10. Sandra and Ramon are students.

2.4.a 1. joven 2. gordo 3. delgado, flaco 4. feliz 5. triste 6. bonita 7. feo 8. joven 9. viejo 10. saludable 11. enfermo 12. cansado

2.4.b 1. tall 2. short 3. young 4. old 5. thin 6. heavy 7. handsome 8. beautiful

2.4.c 1. bad 2. lazy 3. heavy 4. beautiful/pretty/handsome 5. thin 6. happy 7. short 8. ugly 9. sick 10. sad 11. tall 12. ugly 13. good 14. hardworking 15. healthy 16. old

2.4.d Las respuestas dependen del estudiante.

2.5.a 1a. ~~My sisters are sads.~~ 2b. ~~They are intelligents.~~ 3a. ~~We are olds.~~ 4b. ~~The girls are beautifuls.~~ 5a. ~~The dogs are uglys.~~ 6b. ~~My father is youngs.~~

2.5.b 1. The girls are tired. 2. The teachers are happy. 3. The doctors are handsome. 4. The nurses are hardworking. 5. The lawyers are intelligent. 6. The waiters are young. 7. The engineers are beautiful. 8. The cooks are thin.

2.5.c 1. Martha is young. 2. The students are intelligent. 3. Martin is heavy. 4. The gardeners are sick. 5. I am tired. 6. The teacher is pretty/beautiful. 7. The cashiers are lazy. 8. The babysitters are happy. 9. The lawyers are hardworking. 10. I am tall. 11. Ernesto is old. 12. Luis is young.

2.6.a 1. blue 2. red 3. white 4. black 5. orange 6. purple 7. brown 8. yellow 9. green

2.6.b 1. it 2. he 3. it 4. she 5. she 6. he 7. it 8. it 9. he 10. she 11. it 12. it

2.6.c 1. It is red. 2. It is black and white. 3. She is tired. 4. It is expensive. 5. It is blue. 6. He is tall. 7. It is green. 8. She is happy. 9. It is dirty. 10. It is yellow and purple.

2.6.d 1a. ~~Is big.~~ 2b. ~~Is a book.~~ 3b. ~~Is from New York.~~ 4a. ~~Is a doctor.~~ 5a. ~~Is a student.~~ 6b. ~~Is new.~~

2.7.a 1. new 2. ugly 3. expensive 4. old 5. small 6. sad 7. short 8. white 9. big 10. heavy

2.7.b 1. it 2. they 3. it 4. they 5. she 6. they 7. they 8. they 9. they 10. he 11. they 12. it 13. she 14. they 15. they

2.7.c 1. It 2. They 3. It 4. They 5. It 6. They

2.7.d 1. The book is new. It is interesting. 2. The house is big. It is beautiful. 3. The dresses are expensive. They are from Paris. 4. The car is old. It is broken. 5. The chair is orange. It is ugly.

2.8.a 1. This 2. These 3. This 4. This 5. These 6. That 7. That 8. Those 9. That 10. Those

2.8.b 1b. ~~These dress is beautiful.~~ 2b. ~~These boy is my brother.~~ 3a. ~~These book is good.~~ 4b. ~~That boys are from Laos.~~ 5a. ~~That girls are my daughter.~~ 6a. ~~These pencil is broken.~~ 7b. ~~Those teacher is hardworking.~~ 8a. ~~That textbooks are heavy.~~

2.8.c 1. This house is clean. 2. These houses are beautiful/pretty. 3. That store is big. 4. Those tables are cheap. 5. That man is very tall. 6. This dictionary is good. 7. Those backpacks are expensive. 8. This book is interesting. 9. This woman is a teacher. 10. Those children are big.

2.9.a 1. we 2. they 3. we 4. we 5. they 6. we 7. they 8. they 9. she 10. we 11. they 12. they 13. they 14. we 15. she 16. we 17. they 18. they 19. they 20. he

English Grammar Step by Step 1

2.9.b 1. We 2. They 3. They 4. We 5. They 6. They 7. We 8. We

2.9.c 1a. ~~Bob and I we are from Reno.~~ 2b. ~~Lisa and I we are from Leon.~~ 3a. ~~We from Seattle.~~ 4b. ~~We doctors.~~ 5a. ~~Are students.~~ 6a. ~~Sam and I we are tired.~~ 7a. ~~I and Bruce are in love.~~ 8b. ~~Max and I we are doctors.~~

P2.a 1. a chair 2. an egg 3. an apple 4. a table 5. an artist 6. a car 7. a student 8. an orange 9. an engineer 10. a job 11. a nurse 12. an opera

P2.b 1. a 2. a 3. an 4. an 5. a 6. an 7. a 8. an 9. a 10. a 11. a 12. a 13. a 14. an

P2.c 1b. ~~These books is good.~~ 2a. ~~Bob and Al they are tired.~~ 3b. ~~That pens are blue.~~ 4b. ~~Lucy and I we are happy.~~ 5b. ~~These pens is new.~~ 6b. ~~The boys they are at school.~~ 7a. ~~That boy he is tall.~~ 8a. ~~Max is teacher.~~ 9b. ~~They are tireds.~~ 10a. ~~My sister she is beautiful.~~

P2.d 1. A 2. N 3. N 4. A 5. A 6. N 7. N 8. A 9. A 10. N 11. A 12. N 13. A 14. A 15. N 16. N 17. N 18. N 19. N 20. N 21. A 22. A 23. N 24. A

P2.e 1. good 2. expensive 3. thin 4. ugly 5. dirty 6. happy 7. short 8. healthy 9. new 10. white 11. hardworking 12. tall 13. sad 14. heavy

P2.f 1. <u>It</u> is new. 2. <u>She</u> is tall. 3. <u>They</u> are beautiful. 4. <u>They</u> are from Bolivia. 5. <u>They</u> are blue and white. 6. <u>It</u> is broken. 7. <u>We</u> are short. 8. <u>It</u> is yellow. 9. <u>They</u> are tired. 10. <u>We</u> are hardworking. 11. <u>It</u> is purple. 12. <u>They</u> are small.

P2.g 1. is 2. are 3. are 4. are 5. is 6. is 7. are 8. are 9. are 10. am 11. are 12. are

P2.h 1. It is new. 2. They are old. 3. She is intelligent. 4. He is nice. 5. They are expensive.

P2.i 1. Susan and I are tired. 2. Enrique and I are from Columbia. 3. They are nurses. 4. These cars are new. 5. Lucy and I are hardworking. 6. Raoul is an artist. 7. This dictionary is good. 8. These students are intelligent. 9. Laura and I are from Argentina. We are engineers. 10. The chair and the table are new. They are

expensive. 11. Those dresses are beautiful/pretty. They are from Paris. 12. María and Justin are from Sinaloa. They are in love.

Chapter 3

3.1.a 1. I'm 2. you're 3. he's 4. she's 5. it's 6. we're 7. they're

3.1.b 1. <u>I'm</u> a babysitter. 2. <u>She's</u> from Brazil. 3. <u>It's</u> expensive. 4. <u>They're</u> healthy. 5. <u>He's</u> my father. 6. <u>You're</u> a nurse. 7. <u>I'm</u> lazy. 8. <u>We're</u> old.

3.1.c 1. They<u>'re</u> 2. He<u>'s</u> 3. We<u>'re</u> 4. I<u>'m</u> 5. She<u>'s</u> 6. It<u>'s</u> 7. We<u>'re</u> tired. 8. They<u>'re</u> 9. I<u>'m</u> 10. She<u>'s</u> 11. They<u>'re</u> 12. We<u>'re</u>

3.1.d 1. She's thin. 2. He's an engineer. 3. They're doctors. 4. I'm lazy. 5. She's from Guadalajara. 6. They're heavy.

3.2.a 1. A 2. N 3. A 4. N 5. A 6. N 7. N 8. A 9. N 10. A

3.2.b 1. I am not happy. 2. She is not tired. 3. We are not from Los Angeles. 4. They are not students. 5. Angi is not a doctor. 6. Barbara is not beautiful. 7. The table is not new. 8. My brother is not from Japan. 9. The nurses are not sick. 10. The girls are not from the United States. 11. The backpack is not blue. 12. The dresses are not dirty.

3.2.c 1. The car is not new. 2. Ernesto is not from Lima. 3. The students are not hardworking. 4. Luis and I are not students. 5. Angela is not a cashier. She is a waitress/She's a waitress. 6. Daniel is not a cashier. He is a waiter/He's a waiter. 7. Marco is not sick. He is healthy./He's healthy. 8. I am not from New York. I am from Houston/I'm from Houston.

3.3.a 1. is 2. is not 3. is 4. is not 5. is not 6. is 7. is not 8. is 9. is 10. is not 11. is not 12. is 13. is 14. is

3.3.b   1a. ~~I no a doctor.~~   2a. ~~She no is artist.~~
3b. ~~Caroline no is heavy.~~   4b. ~~Luis is no from Reno.~~   5a. ~~Tom no is a student.~~   6a. ~~They no are in love.~~   7b. ~~We no from Paris.~~   8a. ~~She no is a artist.~~

3.3.c   1. I am not tired.   2. Angi is not from the U.S.
3. I am not sick.   4. The girls are not students.
5. The car is not broken.

3.4.a   1. I'm not lazy.   2. You aren't lazy.   3. He isn't lazy.   4. She isn't lazy.   5. We aren't lazy.   6. They aren't lazy.   7. It isn't expensive.
8. The student isn't from Tijuana.   9. The book isn't new.   10. I'm not a homemaker.

3.4.b   1. isn't   2. I'm   3. isn't   4. aren't   5. aren't
6. isn't   7. I'm   8. aren't   9. isn't

3.4.c   1. isn't   2. is   3. is   4. is   5. isn't   6. isn't   7. isn't
8. is   9. isn't   10. is   11. isn't   12. is

3.5.a   1a. ?   1b. Q   2a. .   2b. S   3a. ?   3b. Q   4a. ?
4b. Q   5a. .   5b. S   6a. ?   6b. Q   7a. ?   7b. Q
8a. .   8b. S

3.5.b   1. Are   2. Are   3. Is   4. Is   5. Is   6. Is   7. Are
8. Is   9. Are   10. Are   11. Are   12. Is   13. Are
14. Are   15. Is   16. Is   17. Is   18. Are

3.5.c   1. Is she tired?   2. Is he happy?   3. Are they doctors?   4. Is the book good?   5. Is Lourdes an engineer?   6. Are we late?   7. Are you a waitress?   8. Are they lawyers?

3.6.a   Las respuestas dependen del estudiante.

3.6.b   1a. ~~Yes, I'm.~~   2b. ~~. Yes, I'm.~~   3a. ~~No, I not.~~
4b. ~~No, I no.~~   5a. ~~Yes, I, am.~~   6a. ~~No, I not.~~
7b. ~~Yes, am.~~   8b. ~~. No, I no.~~   9a. ~~Yes, I'm~~
10b. ~~No I'm not.~~

3.7.a   1. Yes, he is.   2. No, he isn't.   3. Yes, she is.
4. No, she isn't.   5. Yes, he is.   6. No, he isn't.
7. No, she isn't.   8. Yes, she is.

3.7.b   1. Yes, she is.   2. No, she isn't.   3. Yes, she is.
4. No, she isn't.   5. Yes, she is.

3.7.c   1a. ~~Yes, I'm.~~   2b. ~~Yes it is.~~   3b. ~~Yes, she is.~~
4a. ~~Yes, he is.~~   5b. ~~Yes, she's.~~   6b. b. Yes, I am.
7b. ~~Yes, I am.~~   8a. ~~No, I'm not.~~   9a. ~~No, it isn't.~~

P3.a   1. he's   2. you're   3. she's   4. we're   5. they're
6. it's   7. I'm

P3.b   1. <u>I'm</u> in love.   2. <u>She's</u> from Mazatlan.   3.
<u>We're</u> tired.   4. <u>She's</u> from Chile.   5. <u>They're</u>
nurses.   6. <u>It's</u> yellow.   7. <u>They're</u> broken.
8. <u>They're</u> sick.   9. <u>We're</u> in love.   10. <u>He's</u>
short.

P3.c   1. he isn't   2. you aren't   3. she isn't   4. we aren't   5. they aren't   6. it isn't   7. I'm not

P3.d   1a. ~~I no a waitress.~~   2b. ~~She isn,t from San Diego.~~   3b. ~~Ramon isn't sick.~~   4b. ~~Yes, I'm.~~
5a. ~~Tom no is in love.~~   6a. ~~They is not from Texas.~~   7b. ~~Luis no is happy.~~   8a. ~~He no is a artist.~~

P3.e   1a. Are   1b. No, I'm not.   2a. Are   2b. No, I'm
not.   3a. Is   3b. No, he isn't.   4a. Is   4b. No,
she isn't.   5a. Is   5b. No, he isn't.   6a. Is
6b. No, it isn't.   7a. Are   7b. No, they aren't.
8a. Is   8b. No, it isn't.

P3.f   1a. I am not from New York.   1b. I'm not
from New York.   2a. She is not tired.   2b. She
isn't tired.   3a. Adam is not a gardener.
3b. Adam isn't a gardener.   4a. The car is not
dirty.   4b. The car isn't dirty.   5a. We are not
happy.   5b. We aren't happy.   6a. The chairs
are not new.   6b. The chairs aren't new.

P3.g   1. Yes, he is.   2. No, she isn't.   3. No, she isn't.
4. Yes, they are.   5. Yes, they are.   6. No, he
isn't.   7. Yes, he is.   8. Yes, she is.   9. No, she
isn't.   10. Yes, he is.   Yes, it is.

P3.h   1. He is sick.   2. They are young.   3. They are
babysitters.   4. They are from Jalisco.
5. Juana is hardworking.   6. They are from
Buenos Aires.   7. He is a gardener.   8. They
are lawyers.

P3.i   1. Is he happy?   2. Are they happy?   3. Are
they gardeners?   4. Are the boys from Jalisco?
5. Is Lourdes a nurse?   6. Are they from El
Salvador?   7. Is he a waiter?   8. Are they
lawyers?

P3.j   1. He's a waiter. 2. Angela isn't a waitress.
3. Daniela isn't heavy. 4. They're from Santa
Fe. 5. He's intelligent. 6. I'm sick. 7. Jose
and I aren't from Canada. 8. The table isn't
purple. 9. We aren't friends. 10. They're
married. 11. I'm not from Michoacan.
12. The car isn't cheap.

Chapter 4

4.1.a   1. have 2. have 3. has 4. has 5. has 6. have
7. have 8. have 9. have 10. has 11. have
12. has 13. have 14. have 15. have 16. have
17. has 18. have

4.1.b   1. six 2. three 3. five 4. eight 5. two 6. one
7. four 8. seven 9. ten 10. nine

4.1.c   1. have 2. has 3. has 4. have 5. have 6. has
7. have 8. have 9. has 10. have 11. have
12. have 13. has 14. have 15. has 16. has
17. have 18. has

4.2.a   1. He has one pencil. 2. He has two
notebooks. 3. He has two pens. 4. He has
one eraser. 5. He has one dictionary.

4.2.b   1. have a 2. has an 3. has a 4. has a 5. has
an 6. have an 7. have a 8. has a

4.2.c   1b. I have car. 2a. Maria has a books. 3a. I
have orange. 4b. We have teacher. 5a. Leo
has four eraser. 6b. Laura has a egg. 7b. I
have problem. 8b. Lisa has two job. 9b. The
boys have bicycle. 10a. We have friend in
Chicago.

4.2.d   1. I have three cats. 2. I have three pencils.
3. Laura has a backpack. 4. Sam has two
jobs. 5. The student has four textbooks.
6. Carlos has a sister and five brothers.

4.3.a   1. cherries 2. boxes 3. parties 4. cities
5. classes 6. friends 7. churches 8. stores
9. dresses 10. cats 11. kisses 12. boys
13. peaches 14. babies 15. chairs 16. toys
17. ladies 18. nurses 19. sisters 20. watches

4.3.b   1. has 2. are 3. is 4. has 5. is 6. has 7. has
8. is 9. are 10. are

4.3.c   1. The boxes are heavy. 2. I have three
sisters 3. Those oranges are big. 4. The

churches are beautiful. 5. She has two babies.
6. These toys are broken. 7. The peaches are
bad. 8. Lillian has the keys.

4.4.a   1. men 2. people 3. teeth 4. children 5. feet
6. women

4.4.b   1. person 2. tooth 3. woman 4. man 5. foot
6. child

4.4.c   1. the child 2. a man 3. the man 4. the men
5. the teeth 6. the tooth 7. the people 8. the
person 9. a person 10. the women 11. the
woman 12. a woman

4.4.d   1. children 2. child 3. woman 4. man
5. woman 6. people 7. woman 8. children
9. feet 10. man 11. feet 12. tooth
13. children 14. man 15. boys 16. men
17. children 18. women

4.5.a   1. has 2. have 3. have 4. have 5. has 6. has
7. have 8. have 9. has 10. has

4.5.b   1a. I have a dress new. 2b. Ana has a house
beautiful. 3a. The school has chairs blue.
4b. I have a boss good. 5a. I have eyes of
color blue. 6a. Ana has hair straight. 7b. She
has two new dress. 8a. We have goods
teachers.

4.5.c   1. have an 2. has a 3. have a 4. has a 5. has
an 6. have an 7. have a 8. have a

4.5.d   1. He has a white car. 2. Susan has a new
book. 3. We have friends from Chicago.
4. My sister has black eyes. 5. He has a black
cat. 6. I have short hair. 7. You have an
intelligent sister.

4.6.a   1. D 2. B 3. F 4. C 5. A 6. E 7. G

4.6.b   1. has 2. are 3. have 4. are 5. is 6. have
7. are 8. is 9. have 10. is 11. are 12. has
13. are 14. has 15. are 16. are 17. has
18. have 19. is 20. has

4.6.c   1. Conci is sick. 2. Lillian has a new dress.
3. He has two jobs. 4. The house is clean.
5. My boyfriend is handsome. 6. Elvira
has an old car. 7. Enrique and I have two
daughters. 8. The men are lazy.

4.7.a 1. twenty-two 2. forty-one 3. sixty-two 4. fifty-four 5. seventy 6. sixteen 7. fifty-eight 8. twelve 9. eighteen 10. fourteen 11. nineteen 12. eighty-four 13. ninety 14. eleven 15. thirteen 16. thirty-four 17. ninety-nine 18. one hundred 19. forty 20. seventy-seven

4.7.b 1a. ~~Lucas has 24 years.~~ 2a. ~~I have 19 years old.~~ 3b. ~~We have 44.~~ 4b. ~~The women is 37 years old.~~ 5b. ~~I am 22 years.~~ 6a. ~~That man is 97 years.~~ 7b. ~~Lynn and I have 34.~~ 8a. ~~I have 17.~~

4.7.c 1. He is 20 years old. 2. He is 16 years old. 3. They are 19 years old. 4. She is 17 years old. 5. They are 18 years old.

P4.a 1. has 2. have 3. has 4. have 5. have 6. has 7. has 8. have 9. has 10. have 11. have 12. has 13. have 14. has 15. have

P4.b 1. S 2. P 3. S 4. S 5. S 6. P 7. P 8. P 9. P 10. P 11. S 12. S

P4.c 1. twenty-two 2. forty-three 3. sixty-five 4. eighty-six 5. eleven 6. ninety-one 7. eighty-five 8. thirty 9. forty-nine 10. fourteen 11. eighteen 12. eighty-six 13. sixty-four 14. seventy-seven 15. thirty-six 16. thirty-four 17. fifty-five 18. one hundred 19. ninety 20. forty-seven

P4.d 1. parties 2. cities 3. dresses 4. men 5. classes 6. girls 7. churches 8. children 9. aunts 10. boys 11. kisses 12. peaches 13. ladies 14. babies 15. feet 16. erasers 17. teeth 18. notebooks 19. women 20. cherries

P4.e 1a. ~~I have a two sisters.~~ 2b. ~~Maria has nice house.~~ 3a. ~~I have a apple.~~ 4b. ~~We have a teacher good.~~ 5a. ~~Juan has four textbook.~~ 6b. ~~Laura has dresses beautiful.~~ 7a. ~~I have a problem big.~~ 8b. ~~Lisa has three dog.~~ 9b. ~~I have healthy.~~ 10a. ~~They have friend in Utah.~~ 11a. ~~The childs are tired.~~ 12b. ~~The men have sick.~~ 13b. ~~He's a boy good.~~ 14a. ~~She has 16 years.~~ 15b. ~~The womens are from NY.~~

P4.f 1. has 2. are 3. has 4. are 5. has 6. have 7. is 8. are 9. has 10. have 11. is 12. has 13. am 14. have 15. has 16. is

P4.g 1. Susan <u>is</u> thirty years old. 2. Marco <u>is</u> 24 years old. 3. Angel and Lupita <u>have</u> three children. 4. I am <u>not</u> in love. 5. We have a <u>sick</u> <u>daughter</u>. 6. Anna <u>is</u> 14 years old. 7. Linda and I <u>are</u> happy. 8. The men <u>are not</u> from Cuba.

P4.h 1. He's 55 years old. 2. No, he isn't. 3. He's a gardener. 4. He's 10 years old. 5. She's 8 years old. 6. She's 12 years old. 7. Yes, he is. 8. No, he isn't. 9. No, he isn't. 10. He's from El Salvador.

Chapter 5

5.1.a 1. brother. 2. father 3. uncle 4. husband 5. son 6. grandmother 7. grandson 8. nephew

5.1.b 1. mother 2. wife 3. sister 4. grandmother 5. niece 6. granddaughter 7. aunt 8. daughter

5.1.c 1. my sister 2. my sisters 3. my brother 4. my brothers 5. my aunt 6. my aunts 7. my parents 8. my uncle 9. my cousin 10. my cousin

5.1.d 1. My aunt is from San Francisco. 2. My cousin has black eyes. 3. My sisters are from Guadalajara. 4. My children are intelligent. My sons are intelligent. 5. My grandmother is old. 6. My husband has black hair. 7. My friends have a new car. 8. My granddaughters are hardworking. 9. My aunt is from Lima. 10. My nephew is a cashier.

5.2.a 1. Her 2. Her 3. My 4. His 5. His 6. My 7. Her 8. His 9. His 10. Her 11. Her 12. My

5.2.b 1. My 2. Her 3. His 4. His

5.2.c 1. He 2. His 3. He 4. He 5. His 6. His

5.2.d 1. She 2. She 3. Her 4. She 5. Her 6. Her

5.2.e 1. His house is clean. 2. Her house is clean. 3. His car is dirty. 4. Her car is dirty. 5. Her teacher is very pretty.

5.3.a 1. Our 2. Our 3. Your 4. His 5. My 6. His 7. Your 8. Her

5.3.b 1. Our 2. We 3. You 4. Our 5. We 6. You 7. We 8. Your

5.3.c 1. You're 2. You're 3. You're 4. You're 5. your 6. Your

5.3.d 1. Your nephew is handsome. 2. Your garden is pretty. 3. Her daughters are intelligent. 4. Your cousins are from Dallas. 5. Juan and I are tired. Our jobs are difficult. 6. Cecilia and I are friends. Our mothers are friends also.

5.4.a 1. Their 2. Their 3. His 4. Her 5. Their 6. Her 7. Their 8. Her 9. His 10. Her

5.4.b 1. their 2. They 3. They 4. Her 5. His 6. Their 7. Their 8. He

5.4.c 1. They're 2. They're 3. They're 4. Their 5. Their 6. Their

5.4.d 1. Anna and Mario have a house. Their house is pretty. 2. My cousins have a garden. Their garden is pretty/beautiful. 3. My aunt and uncle have a car. Their car is broken. 4. My parents have a big house. Their house is in Michoacan.

5.5.a 1. His full name is Juan Garcia Castro. 2. His first name is Juan. 3. His middle name is Garcia. 4. His last name is Castro. 5. His middle initial is G. 6. Her full name is Patricia Ortiz Sanchez. 7. Her first name is Patricia. 8. Her middle name is Ortiz. 9. Her last name is Sanchez. 10. Her middle initial is O. 11-15. Las respuestas dependen del estudiante.

5.5.b 1. your 2. name 3. I'm 4. years 5. job 6. a 7. you 8. am

P5.a 1a. feminine 1b. uncle 2a. masculine 2b. daughter 3a. masculine 3b. sister 4a. feminine 4b. grandfather 5a. masculine 5b. niece.

P5.b 1. My 2. My 3. Her 4. My 5. His 6. His 7. Their 8. Its 9. Our

P5.c 1. Our 2. Their 3. My 4. Her 5. Our 6. His 7. Their 8. Her

P5.d 1. Her 2. She 3. His 4. She 5. I 6. Your

P5.e 1b. His car is red. 2a. Her jacket is red. 3b. Her daughter is tired. 4a. His uncle is healthy. 5b. My car is new. 6b. His dress is green. 7b. Her brother is handsome. 8a. Their dog is brown. 9b. Their family is big. 10b. Her daughter is sick.

P5.f 1. We have a white car. 2. Our niece is from Madrid. 3. My grandmother has a big house. 4. My sister has blue eyes. 5. His last name is Marquez. 6. Our job is difficult. 7. The doctor is from Chicago. His name is Paul. 8. The teacher is from New York. Her name is Louisa.

P5.g

IDENTIFICATION CARD 2	
First Name	Luis
Middle Initial	J.
Last Name	Alvarez
Street Address	15 First Avenue
City	Placerville
State	Georgia Zip 32333
Telephone Number	(646) 644-1245
Age	24

IDENTIFICATION CARD 3	
First Name	Cynthia
Middle Initial	M.
Last Name	Fox
Street Address	576 University Ave.
City	White Plains
State	New York Zip 10605
Telephone Number	(924) 655-1246
Age	31

Appendix B: Negative Contractions

In Chapter 3 you learned about the negative contractions **aren't** and **isn't**. The following table shows you another way to make contractions in negative sentences that include the verb **to be**.

Contractions with the verb **to be**	
I + **am** followed by **not**	**I'm not**
you + **are** followed by **not**	**you're not**
we + **are** followed by **not**	**we're not**
they + **are** followed by **not**	**they're not**
he + **is** followed by **not**	**he's not**
she + **is** followed by not	**she's not**
it + **is** followed by not	**it's not**

The following table shows both of the contractions available to you when using the verb **to be** in a negative sentence. Notice that, with the exception of **I**, there are two contractions to choose from for each pronoun and that both contractions mean exactly the same thing.

Negative sentences without contractions	Negative sentences with contractions
I am not tired. (No estoy cansado.)	**I'm not tired.** (No estoy cansado.)
You are not tired. (No estás cansado.)	**You're not tired. You aren't tired.** (No estás cansado.)
He is not tired. (Él no está cansado.)	**He's not tired. He isn't tired.** (Él no está cansado.)
She is not tired. (Ella no está cansada.)	**She's not tired. She isn't tired.** (Ella no está cansada.)
We are not tired. (Nosotros no estamos cansados.)	**We're not tired. We aren't tired.** (Nosotros no estamos cansados.)
They are not tired. (Ellos no están cansados.)	**They're not tired. They aren't tired.** (Ellos no están cansados.)

Glossary of Grammar Terms

adjective: A word that modifies or describes a noun or pronoun. **Handsome** (guapo), **pretty** (bonita) and **blue** (azul) are examples of adjectives.

article: A word that is placed before a noun. In English the articles are **the** (el, la, los and las) and **a** and **an** (un and una).

contraction: A word that is formed by combining two other words. Al and del are contractions in Spanish. **I'm** and **isn't** are examples of contractions in English.

demonstrative adjective: An adjective that points out whether something is near by or far away. In English, the demonstrative adjectives are **this, that, these** and **those**.

gender: A type of classification that defines nouns, pronouns and adjectives as masculine, feminine or neuter. Casa is a feminine noun; techo is a masculine noun. In English, gender only applies to a few nouns such as **mother** and **father**.

noun: A person, place, animal or thing. **Teacher** (maestra), **book** (libro) and **park** (parque) are examples of nouns.

plural noun: A noun that refers to more than one person, place, animal, or thing. **Books** (libros) is an example of a plural noun.

possessive adjective: An adjective that shows that something belongs to or is related to a noun. **My** (mi, mis) is an example of a possessive adjective.

preposition: A word that describes time, place, direction, or location. **Over** (arriba de) and **next to** (al lado de) are examples of prepositions.

pronoun: A word that takes the place of a noun. (See *subject pronoun.*)

singular noun: A noun that refers to one person, place, animal or thing. **Book** (libro) is an example of a singular noun.

subject pronoun: A pronoun that is the subject of a sentence. In English, the subject pronouns are **I, you, he, she, it, we** and **they**.

subject: The word or words in the sentence that tell who or what the sentence is about. The subject is usually the first noun or pronoun in the sentence.

verb: A word that show action or state of being. **To be** (ser and estar) and **to have** (tener) are the most common verbs.

Index

English Grammar Step by Step 1

English/Spanish Dictionary

A

address *(ádres)*	dirección
adjective *(ádshetiv)*	adjetivo
afraid *(to be) (tu bi afréid)*	tener miedo
age *(éish)*	edad
airplane *(érplein)*	avión
also *(ólsou)*	también
am *(am)*	soy, estoy
an *(an)*	un, una
and *(and)*	y
apple *(apl)*	manzana
architect *(árquetect)*	arquitecto(a)
are *(ar)*	eres, somos, son, estás, estamos, están
artist *(ártist)*	artista
at *(at)*	a, en
aunt *(ant)*	tía

B

baby *(béibi)*	bebé(a)
babysitter *(béibisiter)*	niñera
backpack *(bákpak)*	mochila
bad *(bad)*	malo(a)
bag *(bag)*	bolsa
ball *(bol)*	pelota
be (verb) *(bi)*	ser, estar
beautiful *(biútiful)*	hermoso(a)
because *(bicós)*	porque
big *(big)*	grande
black *(blak)*	negro(a)
blue *(blu)*	azul
book *(buk)*	libro
boss *(bos)*	jefe(a)
box *(box)*	caja
boy *(bói)*	niño
boyfriend *(bóifrend)*	novio
brother *(bráder)*	hermano
brother-in-law *(bráder in loh)*	cuñado
brown *(bráun)*	café, marrón, castaño

C

call (verb) *(col)*	llamar
car *(car)*	carro, coche, auto
cashier *(cashíer)*	cajero(a)
cat *(cat)*	gato(a)
chair *(cher)*	silla
cheap *(chip)*	barato(a)
cherry *(chérri)*	cereza
child *(cháild)*	niño(a)
city *(síti)*	ciudad
class *(clas)*	clase
clean *(clin)*	limpio(a)
coffee *(cófi)*	
cold (adj.) *(cóuld)*	frío(a)
cold (noun) *(cóuld)*	frío, resfriado
color *(cólor)*	color
complete *(complít)*	completo(a)
complete name *(complít néim)*	nombre completo
consonant *(cónsonant)*	consonante
construction worker *(constrókshon uérker)*	albañil
cook *(cuk)*	cocinero(a)
country *(cóntri)*	país
cousin *(cásin)*	primo(a)
curly *(kérli)*	rizado

D

daughter *(dóter)*	hija
daughter-in-law *(dóter in loh)*	nuera
dictionary *(díkshonari)*	diccionario
dirty *(dérti)*	sucio(a)
divorced *(divórst)*	divorciado(a)
doctor *(dóctor)*	médico(a)
dog *(dog)*	perro(a)
dress *(dres)*	vestido

E

egg *(eg)*	huevo
eight *(éit)*	ocho
eighteen *(éitin)*	dieciocho
eighty *(éiti)*	ochenta
eleven *(iléven)*	once
engineer *(inshenír)*	ingeniero(a)
eraser *(irréiser)*	borrador

expensive (expénsif)	caro(a)		**have** (jav)	tengo, tienes, tenemos, tienen
eye (ái)	ojo		**he** (ji)	él

F

father (fáder)	padre
father-in-law (fáder in loh)	suegro
fear (fir)	miedo
feet (fit)	pies
fifteen (fíftin)	quince
fifty (fífti)	cincuenta
first (ferst)	primero(a)
first name (ferst néim)	primer nombre
five (fáiv)	cinco
foot (fut)	pie
forty (fórti)	cuarenta
four (for)	cuatro
fourteen (fórtin)	catorce
friend (frend)	amigo(a)
from (from)	de, desde

G

garden (gárdn)	jardín
gardener (gárdner)	jardinero(a)
girl (guerl)	niña
girlfriend (guérlfrend)	novia
good (gud)	bueno(a)
grandchild (grancháild)	nieto(a)
granddaughter (grandóter)	nieta
grandfather (granfáder)	abuelo
grandmother (granmáder)	abuela
grandparent (grandpérent)	abuelo
grandson (grandsán)	nieto
gray (gréi)	gris
green (grin)	verde

H

hair (jer)	pelo, cabello
handsome (jánsom)	guapo
happy (jápi)	feliz, contento(a)
hardworking (jarduérkin)	trabajador(a)
has (jas)	tiene

have (jav)	tengo, tienes, tenemos, tienen
he (ji)	él
he's (he is) (jis)	él es, él está
healthy (jélzi)	saludable
heat (jit)	calor
heavy (jévi)	pesado(a)
her (jer)	su (de ella)
his (jis)	su (de él)
homemaker (jomméiker)	ama de casa
hot (jat)	caliente
house (jáus)	casa
how (jáu)	cómo
how old (jáu old)	cuántos años
hundred (jóndred)	cien, ciento
hunger (jánguer)	hambre
hungry (jángri)	hambriento(a)
husband (jásben)	esposo

I

I (ái)	yo
I'm (I am) (áim)	yo soy, yo estoy
identification (aidentifikéishon)	identificación
in (in)	en
in love (in lov)	enamorado(a)
initial (iníshal)	inicial
intelligent (intélishent)	inteligente
interesting (íntrestin)	interesante
is (is)	es, est
it (it)	
it's (its)	

J, K, L

job (shob)	trabajo
key (ki)	llave
kiss (kis)	beso
lady (léidi)	dama
large (larsh)	grande
last name (last néim)	apellido
lawyer (lóier)	abogado(a)
lazy (léisi)	flojo(a), perezoso(a)
love (lov)	amor
luck (lak)	suerte
lucky (láki)	afortunado(a)

M

man *(man)*   hombre

marital status   estado civil
(márital státes)

married *(márid)*   casado(a)

men *(men)*   hombres

middle name?   segundo nombre
(midl néim)

mother *(máder)*   madre

mother-in-law   suegra
(máder in loh)

my *(mái)*   mi, mis

N

name *(néim)*   nombre

nephew *(néfiu)*   sobrino

new *(niú)*   nuevo(a)

nice *(náis)*   agradable

niece *(nis)*   sobrina

nine *(náin)*   nueve

nineteen *(náintin)*   diecinueve

ninety *(náinti)*   noventa

no *(no)*   no

not *(not)*   no

notebook *(nóutbuk)*   cuaderno

noun *(náun)*   sustantivo

number *(námber)*   número

nurse *(ners)*   enfermero(a)

O

occupation   ocupación
(okiupéishon)

of *(of)*   de

old *(old)*   viejo(a)

one *(uán)*   un, uno, una

one hundred   cien, ciento
(uán jòndred)

opera *(ópera)*   ópera

orange *(óransh)*   naranja, anaranjado

our *(áur)*   nuestro(a)

P

parents *(pérents)*   padres

park *(park)*   parque

party *(párti)*   fiesta

peach *(pich)*   durazno

pen *(pen)*   bolígrafo

pencil *(pénsil)*   lápiz

people *(pípl)*   personas, gente

person *(pérson)*   persona

pretty *(príti)*   bonito(a), guapa

problem *(próblem)*   problema

pronoun *(prónaun)*   pronombre

purple *(pérpl)*   morado(a)

Q, R, S

red *(red)*   rojo(a)

relative *(rélativ)*   pariente, familiar

rice *(ráis)*   arroz

sad *(sad)*   triste

salesperson   vendedor(a)
(séilsperson)

school *(skul)*   escuela, colegio

second *(sékond)*   segundo(a)

seven *(séven)*   siete

seventeen *(séventin)*   diecisiete

seventy *(séventi)*   setenta

she *(shi)*   ella

she's (she is) *(shis)*   ella es, ella está

shirt *(shert)*   camisa

short *(short)*   chaparro(a), bajo(a)

sick *(sik)*   enfermo(a)

single *(singl)*   soltero(a)

sister *(síster)*   hermana

sister-in-law   cuñada
(síster in loh)

six *(six)*   seis

sixteen *(síxtin)*   dieciséis

sixty *(síxti)*   sesenta

sleep *(slip)*   sueño

sleepy *(slípi)*   soñoliento

small *(smol)*   pequeño(a)

son *(san)*   hijo

son-in-law *(san in loh)*   yerno

state *(stéit)*   estado

store *(stor)*   tienda

straight *(stréit)*   lacio(a)

student *(stiúdent)*   estudiante

subject *(sóbshekt)*   sujeto

T

table *(téibl)*   mesa

tall *(tol)*   alto(a)

teacher (tícher)	maestro(a)	**white** (uáit)	blanco(a)
teeth (tiz)	dientes	**why** (uái)	por qué
telephone (télefon)	teléfono	**wife** (uáif)	esposa
ten (ten)	diez	**woman** (uéman)	mujer
textbook (tékstbuk)	libro de texto	**women** (uémen)	mujeres
that (dat)	ese, esa, eso	**work (noun)** (uérk)	trabajo
the (de)	la, lo, las, los	**work (verb)** (uérk)	trabajar
their (der)	su (de ellos), su (de ellas), sus (de ellos), sus (de ellas)	**year** (íer)	año
		yellow (iélou)	amarillo(a)
there (der)	allí	**yes** (iés)	sí
these (díis)	estos, estas	**you** (iú)	tú, usted, ustedes
they (déi)	ellos, ellas	**young** (iáng)	joven
they're (they are) (deyr)	ellos son, ellos están, ellas son, ellas están	**your** (iór)	tu, tus, su, sus
		you're (you are) (iúr)	tú eres, tú estás, usted es, usted está, ustedes, son, ustedes están
thin (zin)	delgado(a)		
thirteen (zértin)	trece	**zip code** (tsip cóud)	código posta
thirst (zerst)	sed		
thirsty (zérsti)	sediento(a)		
thirty (zérti)	treinta		
this (dis)	este, esta, esto		
those (dóuz)	esos, esas		
three (zri)	tres		
tired (táierd)	cansado(a)		
to be (tu bi)	ser, estar		
tooth (tuz)	diente		
toy (tói)	juguete		
tree (tri)	árbol		
twelve (tuélf)	doce		
twenty (tuénti)	veinte		
two (tu)	dos		

U, V

ugly (ógli)	feo(a)
uncle (oncl)	tío
verb (verb)	verbo
very (véri)	muy
vowel (váuel)	vocal

W, X, Y, Z

waiter (uéiter)	mesero
waitress (uéitres)	mesera
we (uí)	nosotros, nosotras
we're (we are) (uér)	somos, estamos
weather (uéder)	clima, tiempo
what (uát)	qué, cuál
when (uén)	cuándo
where (uér)	dónde

English Grammar Step by Step 1

Spanish/English Dictionary

A

abogado(a)	lawyer (lóier)
abuela	grandmother (granmáder)
abuelo	grandfather (granfáder) grandparent (grandpérent)
adjetivo	adjective (ádshetiv)
afortunado(a)	lucky (láki)
agradable	nice (náis)
albañil	construction worker (constrókshon uérker)
allí	there (der)
alto(a)	tall (tol)
ama de casa	homemaker (jomméiker)
amarillo(a)	yellow (iélou)
amigo(a)	friend (frend)
amor	love (lov)
año	year (íer)
apellido	last name (last néim)
árbol	tree (tri)
arquitecto(a)	architect (árquetect)
arroz	rice (ráis)
artista	artist (ártist)
avión	airplane (érplein)
azul	blue (blu)

B

bajo(a)	short (short)
barato(a)	cheap (chip)
bebé(a)	baby (béibi)
beso	kiss (kis)
blanco(a)	white (uáit)
bolígrafo	pen (pen)
bolsa	bag (bag)
bonito(a)	pretty (príti) beautiful (biútiful)
borrador	eraser (irréiser)
bueno(a)	good (gud)

C

cabello	hair (jer)
café	coffee (cófi) brown (bráun)
caja	box (box)

cajero(a)	cashier (cashíer)
caliente	hot (jat)
calor	heat (jit)
camisa	shirt (shert)
cansado(a)	tired (táierd)
caro(a)	expensive (expénsif)
carro	car (car)
casa	house (jáus)
casado(a)	married (márid)
castaño	brown (bráun)
catorce	fourteen (fórtin)
cereza	cherry (chérri)
chaparro(a)	short (short)
cien, ciento	hundred (jóndred)
cinco	five (fáiv)
cincuenta	fifty (fífti)
ciudad	city (síti)
clase	class (clas)
clima	weather (uéder)
cocinero(a)	cook (cuk)
código postal	zip code (tsip cóud)
color	color (cólor)
cómo	how (jáu)
completo(a)	complete (complít)
consonante	consonant (cónsonant)
contento(a)	happy (jápi)
cuaderno	notebook (nóutbuk)
cuál	what (uát) which (uích)
cuándo	when (uén)
cuántos años	how old (jáu old)
cuarenta	forty (fórti)
cuatro	four (for)
cuñada	sister-in-law (síster in loh)
cuñado	brother-in-law (bráder in loh)

D

dama	lady (léidi)
de	from (from), of (of)
desde	from (from)
delgado(a)	thin (zin)
diccionario	dictionary (díkshonari)
diecinueve	nineteen (náintin)

dieciocho	eighteen (éitin)
dieciséis	sixteen (síxtin)
diecisiete	seventeen (séventin)
diente	tooth (tuz)
dientes	teeth (tiz)
diez	ten (ten)
dirección	address (ádres)
divorciado(a)	divorced (divórst)
doce	twelve (tuélf)
dónde	where (uér)
dos	two (tu)
durazno	peach (pich)

E

edad	age (éish)
él	he (ji)
el	the (de)
ella	she (shi)
ellas	they (déi)
ellos	they (déi)
en	in (in)
enamorado(a)	in love (in lov)
enfermero(a)	nurse (ners)
enfermo(a)	sick (sik)
eres	are (ar)
es	is (is)
esa	that (dat)
escuela	school (skul)
ese	that (dat)
esos, esas	those (dóuz)
esposa	wife (uáif)
esposo	husband (jásben)
esta	this (dis)
está	is (is)
estado	state (stéit)
estado civil	marital status (márital státes)
estamos	are (ar)
están	are (ar)
estar	to be (tu bi)
estas	these (díis)
estás	are (ar)
este	this (dis)
esto	this (dis)
estos	these (díis)
estoy	am (am)
estudiante	student (stiúdent)

F

feliz	happy (jápi)
feo(a)	ugly (ógli)
fiesta	party (párti)
flojo(a)	lazy (léisi)
frío	cold (noun) (cóuld)
frío(a)	cold (adj.) (cóuld)

G

gato(a)	cat (cat)
gente	people (pípl)
grande	big (big), large (larsh)
gris	gray (gréi)
guapa	pretty (príti), beautiful (biútiful)
guapo	handsome (jánsom)

H

hambre	hunger (jánguer)
hambriento(a)	hungry (jángri)
hermana	sister (síster)
hermano	brother (bráder)
hija	daughter (dóter)
hijo	son (san)
hombre	man (man)
hombres	men (men)
huevo	egg (eg)

I, J, K

identificación	identification (aidentifikéishon)
ingeniero(a)	engineer (inshenír)
inicial	inicial (iníshal)
inteligente	intelligent (intélishent)
interesante	interesting (íntrestin)
jardín	garden (gárdn)
jardinero(a)	gardener (gárdner)
jefe(a)	boss (bos)
joven	young (iáng)
juguete	toy (tói)

L

lacio(a)	straight (stréit)
lápiz	pencil (pénsil)
la	the (de)
las	the (de)
libro	book (buk)

libro de *texto*	textbook *(tékstbuk)*	**nuestro(a)(os)(as)**	our *(áur)*
limpio(a)	clean *(clin)*	**nueve**	nine *(náin)*
llamar	to call *(tu col)*	**nuevo(a)**	new *(niú)*
llave	key *(ki)*	**número**	number *(námber)*
los	the *(de)*		

M

madre	mother *(máder)*
maestro(a)	teacher *(tícher)*
malo(a)	bad *(bad)*
manzana	apple *(apl)*
marrón	brown *(bráun)*
mesera	waitress *(uéitres)*
mesero	waiter *(uéiter)*
médico(a)	doctor *(dóctor)*
mesa	table *(téibl)*
mi	my *(mái)*
miedo	fear *(fir)*
mis	my *(mái)*
mochila	backpack *(bákpak)*
morado	purple *(pérpl)*
marrón	brown *(bráun)*
mujer	woman *(uéman)*
mujeres	women *(uémen)*
muy	very *(véri)*

N

naranja	orange *(óransh)*
negro(a)	black *(blak)*
nieta	grandaughter *(grandóter)* grandchild *(grancháild)*
nieto	grandson *(grandsán)* grandchild *(grancháild)*
niña	gir *(guerl)*, child *(cháild)*
niñera	babysitter *(béibisiter)*
niño	boy *(bói)*, child *(cháild)*
no	no *(no)* not *(not)*
nombre	name *(néim)*
nombre completo	complete name *(complít néim)*
nosotras	we *(uí)*
nosotros	we *(uí)*
noventa	ninety *(náinti)*
novia	girlfriend *(guérlfrend)*
novio	boyfriend *(bóifrend)*
nuera	daughter-in-law *(dóter in loh)*

O, P

ochenta	eighty *(éiti)*
ocho	eight *(éit)*
ocupación	occupation *(okiupéishon)* job *(shob)*
ojo	eye *(ái)*
once	eleven *(iléven)*
ópera	opera *(ópera)*
padre	father *(fáder)*
padres	parents *(pérents)*
país	country *(cóntri)*
pariente	relative *(rélativ)*
parque	park *(park)*
pesado(a)	heavy *(jévi)*
pelo	hair *(jer)*
pelota	ball *(bol)*
pequeño(a)	small *(smol)*
perro(a)	dog *(dog)*
persona	person *(pérson)*
personas	people *(pípl)*
pie	foot *(fut)*
pies	feet *(fit)*
por qué	why *(uái)*
porque	because *(bicós)*
primer(a)(o)	first *(ferst)*
primo(a)	cousin *(cásin)*
problema	problem *(próblem)*
pronombre	pronoun *(prónaun)*

Q, R

qué	what *(uát)*
quince	fifteen *(fíftin)*
resfriado	cold (noun) *(fíftin)*
rizado	curly *(kérli)*
rojo(a)	red *(red)*

S

saludable	healthy *(jélzi)*
sed	thirst *(zérst)*
sediento(a)	thirsty *(zérsti)*
segundo nombre	middle name *(midl néim*

segundo(a)	second (sékond)
seis	six (six)
ser	to be (tu bi)
sesenta	sixty (síxti)
setenta	seventy (séventi)
sí	yes (iés)
siete	seven (séven)
silla	chair (cher)
sobrina	niece (nis)
sobrino	nephew (néfiu)
soltero(a)	single (singl)
somos	are (ar)
son	are (ar)
soñoliento(a)	sleepy (slípi)
soy	am (am)
su (de él)	his (jis)
su (de ella)	her (jer)
su (de ellas)	their (der)
su (de ellos)	their (der)
sucio(a)	dirty (dérti)
suegra	mother-in-law (máder in loh)
suegro	father-in-law (fáder in loh)
sueño	sleep (slip)
suerte	luck (lak)
sujeto	subject (sóbshekt)
sus (de ellas)	their (der)
sus (de ellos)	their (der)
sustantivo	noun (náun)

T

también	also (ólsou)
teléfono	telephone (télefon)
tenemos	have (jav)
tener	to have (to jav)
tengo	have (jav)
tía	aunt (jav)
tiempo	weather (uéder)
tienda	store (stor)
tiene	has (jas)
tienen	have (jav)
tienes	have (jav)
tío	uncle (oncl)
trabajador(a)	hardworking (jarduérkin)
trabajar	to work (verb) (uérk)
trabajo (noun)	work (uérk)

trece	thirteen (zértin)
treinta	thirty (zérti)
tres	three (zri)
triste	sad (sad)
tu	your (iór)
tú	you (iú)
tus	your (iór)

U, V, W, X, Y, Z

un	a (éi), an (an), one (uán)
una	a (éi), an (an), one (uán)
uno	one (uán)
usted	you (iú)
ustedes	you (iú)
veinte	twenty (tuénti)
vendedor(a)	salesperson (séilsperson)
verbo	verb (verb)
verde	green (grin)
vestido	dress (dres)
viejo(a)	old (old)
vocal	vowel (váuel)
y	and (and)
yerno	son-in-law (san in loh)
yo	I (ái), me (mi)

Join the *Paso a Paso* Community

Thank you for purchasing *Gramática del inglés: Paso a paso* or *English Grammar: Step by Step*. We hope that it has made learning (or teaching) English a little bit easier.

We are always working to improve our existing books and also planning new ones. Here are some of the projects we're working on:

- Activity Guides for teachers who are using our books in their classes

- An audio CD to accompany our grammar books

- Grammar activities based on popular music

<u>We also can tell you about quantity discounts available to organizations that want to purchase multiple copies of our books.</u>

If you're interested in learning about these or other topics, send us your contact information. When you write, let us know if you're a student or a teacher. You can

- Email your contact information to **tenayapress@tenaya.com**

- Complete the form below

Contact information for Tenaya Press

Name _____

Street address _____

City, State, Zip _____

Email address _____

Are you a teacher? If so, where do you teach? _____

Send this form to

Tenaya Press

3481 Janice Way

Palo Alto, CA 94303

Made in the USA
Lexington, KY
11 June 2014